Learning with the Sunday Gospels

Part One:
Advent to Pentecost

Learning with the Sunday Gospels

Part One:
Advent to Pentecost

Leslie J. Francis and Diane Drayson

MOWBRAY

Mowbray
A Cassell imprint
Wellington House, 125 Strand, London WC2R 0BB
370 Lexington Avenue, New York, NY 10017-6550
www.cassell.co.uk

First published 1999

British Library Cataloguing-in-Publication Data
A catalogue record for this book is available from the British Library.

ISBN 0-264-67445-6

Worksheets for use with these books will be published later in 1999.

Printed and bound in Great Britain by Redwood Books Ltd.

CONTENTS

Introduction to the Season of Lent   96

Introduction to the Season of Easter   **134**

PREFACE

The Revised Common Lectionary is bringing many of the churches closer together as they share and reflect on common passages of Scripture Sunday by Sunday. One of the strengths of this lectionary is the way in which the distinctive voices of the three synoptic gospels are heard in the year of Matthew, the year of Mark, and the year of Luke. The aim of this book is to make sure that the children of the church are introduced to these gospels alongside the adult worshippers.

As in our earlier programmes for children, the present programme reflects two deeply held personal commitments: commitment to parish ministry and commitment to good quality educational theory and practice.

We are grateful to those congregations with whom we have worked and worshipped for their part in shaping our thinking and practice. We also wish to express our appreciation to the Principal and Governors of Trinity College Carmarthen for fostering and encouraging our work; to Ruth McCurry for commissioning and helping to structure the project; to the Revd Enid Morgan for proposing a Welsh translation of our work; to the Revd Robert Paterson for helping us steer a path through the lectionary; and to Anne Rees for shaping the manuscript.

Leslie J. Francis
Diane Drayson

Centre for Theology and Education
Trinity College Carmarthen
Easter 1998

Learning with the Lectionary

Learning with the Sunday Gospels is a project-based programme of Christian education. It is organized around the gospel readings proposed by the Revised Common Lectionary as adopted by the Church of England and the Church in Wales. The programme is sufficiently flexible to suit the many other churches which are following the same basic lectionary. Its purpose is to develop understanding of biblical themes and to promote a positive attitude towards worship.

This introduction contains three sections. The first section, *Theory*, examines the educational and theological ideas on which the book is based. The second section, *Programme*, describes the structure of the 171 individual chapters. The third section, *Practice*, discusses the different ways in which work among children can be carried out.

THEORY

All-age learning and worship are now central features of the churches' pastoral strategy. Attendance at the Sunday service has come to play an increasingly important part in the Christian education and nurture of the young.

When churches are using the Revised Common Lectionary in the context of all-age learning and worship, this means making the Scripture readings accessible to people of all ages and of various levels of Christian maturity. The present programme begins with the gospel readings from the lectionary.

Learning with the Sunday Gospels has been designed to help clergy, lay ministers and children's work leaders reflect on the themes of the Sunday gospels and to provide examples of how these themes may be developed in church, Sunday school and other contexts of Christian nurture. The programme is committed to all-age participation, concrete images and project learning.

ALL-AGE PARTICIPATION

All-age learning and worship recognizes that all individuals, children and adults alike, come with different experiences, different needs and different ways of expressing themselves. All-age learning and worship needs to take these differences seriously.

All-age learning and worship also recognizes that individual members of the church learn best from each other. Learning is a two-way process. Children learn from adults and adults learn from children. They are travelling together on a shared pilgrimage and are able to enrich and resource each other for the journey.

When children share the theme which the adults are exploring, they can enrich the adults' learning with their fresh insights and enthusiasm. When adults share with children, the adults contribute their rich experience of life.

Because individuals differ so greatly there are times when their learning and worship can best take place in sub-groups able to focus on specialist needs. Workshops or worship sessions for children may provide examples of such subgroups. Because individuals learn from others' differences there are other times when their learning and worship can best take place together.

CONCRETE IMAGES

Learning with the Sunday Gospels sets out to identify one image at the heart of each gospel reading. Then it suggests ways in which children and adults can explore the concrete image at their own level and, through such exploration, gain insight into the gospel theme.

This use of concrete images reflects our view that religious language has its roots in concrete, everyday experiences, which are then changed to enable us to speak about religious realities we are not able totally to grasp. By identifying the concrete image at the core of each Sunday's gospel, it is possible to enable both adults and children to change and develop this image to a level consistent with their own religious maturity.

PROJECT LEARNING

Language acquires its significance from being grounded in human experience. Project learning structures the opportunities for adults and children to experience the concrete images underpinning religious language. Adults and children are encouraged to explore these images at their own level and at their own pace. The fruits of such exploration are then to be shared.

In some cases the concrete image and the religious significance are already closely related in the languages of the Scriptures themselves. For example, both Hebrew and Greek use the same word for 'wind' and 'Holy Spirit'. The wind is an essential concrete image underlying our understanding of God the Holy Spirit. The more we experience and think about the wind, the more we can understand and interpret our experience of the Holy Spirit.

In other cases, it is necessary to search further to find the most appropriate concrete image.

LOCAL PRACTICE

Experience and research show that there is a wide diversity among local churches exploring and implementing good practice in Christian nurture and all-age worship and learning. Churches vary greatly in available resources, commitment, and leadership, as well as in their educational philosophy and theological perspective. For example, some churches integrate children wholly within the main Sunday service, without making any separate provision. Some churches operate special children's groups throughout part of the service every week, throughout the whole service some weeks, or on a Saturday or weekday evening. Some churches operate all-age project days. *Learning with the Sunday Gospels* has been designed as a flexible programme which can be used in a variety of ways. Local churches, therefore, will find themselves using this material in a variety of ways.

PROGRAMME

The two volumes of *Learning with the Sunday Gospels* contain 171 chapters, one for each Sunday of the three-year lectionary cycle. Each chapter identifies a clear concrete image at the heart of the theme of the gospel reading.

Each chapter follows the same structure and is divided into four sections: preparation, exploring with children, exploring with adults, and celebrating together.

PREPARATION

This first section, on preparation, is there to help the leaders deepen their own understanding of the gospel reading and to relate this reading to the project approach to Christian learning.

Gospel theme provides a brief and focused comment on the Scripture reading and shows how the concrete image can help to illuminate this reading.

Aims sets out the intentions of the project programme. At the end of each project the leaders should assess how far the aims have been realized.

EXPLORING WITH CHILDREN

The second section, on exploring with children, provides a variety of ideas and suggestions under four headings. You may choose an idea from each section, or you may choose from only some of the sections. Select the ideas that best suit the needs and interests of your leaders and the children.

Starting offers one specific way to initiate the project. Experienced teachers may prefer to use their own ideas.

Talking points suggests topics which may be developed as appropriate by the teachers and leaders. The best time for this is while the children work. Project activities should be used as springboards for reflection and discussion.

Activities suggests things to create and to do. Some of these activities are best suited for a single, relatively brief session. Other activities are best suited for a series of sessions or a whole-day workshop. Leaders may wish to select one activity for the whole group, or work on different activities with smaller groups.

Display provides suggested headings to make links between project learning and the gospel themes. It is helpful to leave the work on display in the church and to use these brief headings to interpret the display for children and adults. Leaders may wish to provide more extensive introductions to the work.

EXPLORING WITH ADULTS

The third section, on exploring with adults, suggests a method for helping adults to link the concrete image with the gospel theme. The method can be used in weekday house groups to help adults prepare for the Sunday service, or when adults meet together on Sunday before the worship service. The method involves three steps.

Experience invites adults to draw on and to discuss their own experience relevant to the theme.

Gospel invites adults to ask questions of and to reflect on the Sunday gospel.

Application draws together the personal experience with the gospel theme and challenges adults to apply their understanding to the life of their church, their personal lives, and the worship service.

CELEBRATING TOGETHER

The fourth section, on celebrating together, provides suggestions for the worship service.

Welcoming children suggests ways in which the children's activities can be most effectively integrated within the worship service. Time needs to be given to help the children feel that they are contributing to the service and enhancing the quality of the teaching and worship.

Hymns and songs suggests a small selection of hymns and songs relevant to each project theme, selected from the school hymn-book *Come and Praise* and from the church hymn-book *Hymns Ancient and Modern New Standard*. While hymns known best to children from their school hymn-book may be unknown to many adult worshippers, some of the church's traditional hymns may be relatively unknown to many children. It is therefore good to choose from both books.

INDEXES

Cumulative indexes of the images, themes and Scripture readings covered by both volumes of *Learning with the Sunday Gospels* are provided at the end of Part Two.

PRACTICE

Many factors influence how local churches organize their children's work, including patterns of Sunday services, numbers of children, willingness of teachers and leaders and availability of buildings. It is increasingly recognized that the key to effective work among children requires regular contact with the adult congregation. This can be achieved in a range of ways, including weekly withdrawal classes, a monthly pattern of Sunday school and family services, weekday evening sessions, project days and co-operation with church schools. *Learning with the Sunday Gospels* is appropriate for all these contexts but will be used differently in each setting.

WITHDRAWAL CLASSES

Some churches have children present for part of the main service each Sunday. Either they come to the first part of the service and are withdrawn before the sermon, or they begin their own classes separately and join the adults for the second half of the service. These withdrawal classes are likely to be relatively short and it is necessary to focus the lesson with care.

Learning with the Sunday Gospels can be used in two different ways when withdrawal classes are held. Some churches may decide to follow the gospel theme each week. They will select one or two key activities for the children to enjoy and then share these activities with the whole congregation later in the service. Other churches may decide to spend several weeks exploring one gospel theme before sharing it with the congregation on the Sunday when that gospel reading is used in the service.

SUNDAY SCHOOL AND FAMILY SERVICES

Some churches operate their children's work most Sunday mornings separately from the main service, but once a month integrate children and adults for a family service. This model has several advantages. Once a month it lets the main service be more child-centred, while on the other Sundays it lets the adults tailor a service appropriate to their needs and allows more time for the children's work in their own classes.

If a monthly pattern is employed one theme can be developed more fully over three weeks. For the family service the children's project work can be displayed in the church during the previous week, and the service can be developed around the project work.

WEEKDAY EVENING SESSIONS

Some churches organize their children's work through weekday evening sessions. These churches either expect the children to be present at the main Sunday service each week, or arrange a special family service once a month. Either a new project theme can be introduced each week or one theme can be developed over several sessions.

PROJECT DAYS

Some churches do all or part of their children's work through project days or project half-days on a Saturday, during school holidays or at half-term. Project days permit a theme to be explored in depth and may include a wide range of craft, dance, drama and music, as well as special features like outings and field trips. Project days need to relate closely to the main service on the following Sunday, when the children's work can be integrated as they celebrate the climax of their project with the adult congregation.

CHURCH SCHOOLS

Some churches have a close link with a local church school. *Learning with the Sunday Gospels* is ideally suited for church schools which desire to link the general curriculum with the worship of the church. Teachers will identify many ways in which these projects can be promoted across the curriculum and how they can enable individual classes or the whole school to contribute towards the Sunday service in church, as well as to school services.

Introduction to the Season of Advent

Traditionally, for the church the season of Advent is a sombre period of preparation. During the season of Advent the people of God prepare themselves both for the annual celebration of the nativity and for the second coming of the Lord. The second coming strikes the two notes of hope and of judgement.

The gospel readings for the first Sunday of Advent emphasize both the unpredictability of the hour and the sharpness of the judgement. The gospel readings for the second Sunday of Advent concentrate on the theme of the repentance proclaimed by John the Baptist as the proper act of preparation. The gospel readings for the third Sunday of Advent adopt a gentler tone. These readings continue to focus on John the Baptist, but now emphasize his role as forerunner. The gospel readings for the fourth Sunday of Advent move attention to the person of Mary who, in her unique way, prepared for the incarnation.

While the church's calendar properly prepares for Christmas through a season of penitence and repentance, the young people within the churches' congregations are living their lives in a busy secular world, where the mass media, the shops and the schools are preparing for Christmas in a very different kind of way. The church cannot ignore these powerful and pervasive influences on the child.

The aims of the project activities suggested for the four Sundays of Advent, therefore, fully recognize the pervasive influence of the excitement and anticipation which surrounds the child's view of Christmas. Taking the child's secular experience as the starting point, these projects set out to relate these experiences to the themes of the church's lectionary.

1 ADVENT CANDLES

PREPARATION

GOSPEL THEME

Be prepared (Matthew 24.36–44)

This gospel reading is part of Matthew's teaching about the last days. The whole of Matthew 24 is stimulated by the disciples' question, put privately to Jesus, 'What will be the sign of your coming at the end of the age?' There are two parts to the answer given to this question in the present passage. The first part is that no one knows when the end will come. The second part is that the disciples must be awake and prepared for Jesus' coming at any time.

We can begin to experience the significance of the Bible's teaching on the need to be ready and to be prepared by exploring the church's traditions concerning the Advent candles.

AIMS

- to build on our experiences of Advent candles;

- to help us understand how Advent candles prepare for Christmas;

- to see how Advent prepares God's people for the coming of Christ.

EXPLORING WITH CHILDREN

STARTING

Light a candle. For safety, place it in a tray of sand. Darken the room and look at the candle flame. Discuss the candle, drawing out ideas of:

- the thousands of years when this was all the light people had;

- the strength of the light shining in the darkness;

- the beauty of the flame;

- times we use candles today, such as birthdays and special dinners;

- the hope and comfort given by even small lights, such as night-lights in a bedroom.

TALKING POINTS

Tell Jesus' words from Matthew about his second coming. As you work, talk with the children about the significance of candles at Advent. You could include the following points:

- at Advent we remember Jesus' birth and that he will come again;

- the candle is a sign of our hope;

- we light candles to focus our thoughts;

- as we light our candles this year, let us remember Jesus' coming.

ACTIVITIES

- Decorate candles with dried flowers or stickers or paper. Heat a spoon under hot water. Press the spoon to the candle to soften the wax slightly and then add the decorations.

- Work together to make and decorate the Advent wreath for the church. Before the activity session you will need to determine the location for the wreath and the size required, and you will need to have made the base. Together attach the candles and decorate with greenery.

- Make table decorations in the shape of a candle. Cover cardboard squares and cardboard cylinders (such as clingfilm rolls cut in thirds) in foil paper. Attach the cylinders to the base with Plasticine. Cut a 'flame' for the top.

- Make clay candleholders. Paint when dry.

DISPLAY

- Today's theme is preparing for Christmas.
- Advent candles are a sign of hope.
- At Advent we remember Jesus' birth.
- At Advent we look forward to Jesus' second coming.
- Our work today is about Advent candles.

EXPLORING WITH ADULTS

EXPERIENCE

- What experiences and feelings do you associate with the Advent candles?

- What do you see as the significance of the single candle burning on Advent Sunday?

- What do you see as the significance of lighting extra candles each Sunday?

GOSPEL

- What does this gospel say about the need for preparation?

- How do you interpret this message for today?

- What does this gospel say about God's coming among men and women?

APPLICATION

- How can your church best proclaim the message of the Advent candles?

- How can you best use the Advent candles?

- How can the Advent candles best be used in the liturgy?

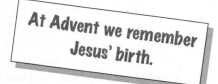
At Advent we remember Jesus' birth.

CELEBRATING TOGETHER

WELCOMING CHILDREN

At an appropriate point in the service, receive the children's Advent candles. Explain how the light of these candles drives away the darkness of unbelief and prepares for Christ's coming at Christmas. Invite a child to light the first of the Advent candles. Other work prepared by the children can be appropriately displayed.

HYMNS AND SONGS

Come and Praise
114 Flick'ring candles in the night
118 When the winter day is dying

Hymns Ancient and Modern New Standard
 28 Lo, he comes with clouds descending
117 Praise to the holiest in the height

2
ADVENT WREATHS

PREPARATION

GOSPEL THEME

Be prepared (Mark 13.24–37)

This gospel reading is part of Mark's apocalyptic discourse, the chapter which separates Jesus' final ministry in Jerusalem from the Passion narrative. After he had left the temple, Peter, James, John and Andrew asked Jesus 'What will be the sign that all these things are about to be accomplished?' Jesus' answer is to advise them to be always on the alert because no one knows the precise time. The season of Advent reminds us today that we, too, need to keep awake and to watch for the Lord's coming.

We can begin to experience the significance of the Bible's teaching on the need to be ready and to be prepared by exploring the significance of the Advent wreaths.

AIMS

- to build on our experiences of Advent wreaths;
- to help us understand how Advent wreaths prepare for Christmas;
- to see how Advent prepares God's people for the coming of Christ.

EXPLORING WITH CHILDREN

STARTING

Show the children an Advent wreath. Ask if they have seen any displayed yet on doors in their neighbourhood. Discuss Advent wreaths, drawing out ideas of:

- whether or not they put up a wreath at home;
- the date when wreaths are put up;
- materials used to make wreaths, for example holly leaves;
- the green of the leaves at a time when most trees are bare;
- the promise of life and hope given in the darkness of winter.

TALKING POINTS

Tell Jesus' words from Mark about his second coming. As you work, talk with the children about the significance of wreaths at this time of Advent. You could include the following points:

- the green leaves remind us that summer will come again;
- at Advent we remember that Jesus will come again;
- the green leaves and Advent are both signs of hope;
- we make wreaths as part of our preparation for Christmas;
- we also prepare ourselves for Jesus' second coming.

ACTIVITIES

- Work together to make a large Advent wreath to decorate the church. Provide a wreath shape made out of wire or bare branches or green florist foam. Provide a variety of green leaves and berries.
- Make small individual wreaths for the children to take home for their bedroom doors.
- Make edible wreaths from marzipan. Colour the marzipan green, roll it and cut out leaves. Attach these to a foil circle with icing.
- Make paper wreaths. Cut leaves from green paper and glue them to a cardboard circle.

DISPLAY

- Today's theme is preparing for Christmas.
- Green leaves give hope of summer.
- Christmas gives hope of Jesus' second coming.
- At Advent we look forward to Jesus' second coming.
- Our work today is about Advent wreaths.

EXPLORING WITH ADULTS

EXPERIENCE

- What experiences and feelings do you associate with Advent wreaths?
- What do you see as the significance of the Advent wreath?
- How does the wreath speak distinctively of Advent rather than Christmas?

GOSPEL

- What does this gospel say about the need to keep awake?
- How do you interpret the message to keep awake for today?
- What does this gospel say about God's expectations for us?

APPLICATION

- How can your church best establish the motif of the Advent wreath?
- How can you best use the Advent wreath?
- How can the Advent wreath best be used in liturgy?

CELEBRATING TOGETHER

WELCOMING CHILDREN

At an appropriate point in the service, receive the children's Advent wreaths. Explain how the Advent wreath becomes a distinctive proclamation of the message of Advent, promising life and hope in a world of winter and darkness. Invite a child to display a wreath prominently in the church. Other work prepared by the children can be appropriately displayed.

HYMNS AND SONGS

Come and Praise
119 The holly and the ivy
141 Shalom, shalom, may peace be with you

Hymns Ancient and Modern New Standard
 25 The advent of our king
 29 The Lord will come and not be slow

3
ADVENT CALENDAR

PREPARATION

GOSPEL THEME

Be prepared (Luke 21.25–36)

This gospel reading is part of Luke's teaching about the last days. The teaching is stimulated by the disciples' question, 'Teacher, when will this be, and what will be the sign that this is about to take place?' Luke's message to the disciples is to be on guard so that day should not catch them unawares. The season of Advent reminds us today that we, too, need to be on guard and to be prepared for the Lord's coming.

We can begin to experience the significance of the Bible's teaching on the need to be on guard and to be actively looking for the coming of Jesus by exploring the Advent calendar.

AIMS

- to build on our experiences of Advent calendars;
- to help us understand how Advent calendars prepare for Christmas;
- to see how Advent prepares God's people for the coming of Christ.

EXPLORING WITH CHILDREN

STARTING

Display an Advent calendar. Talk with the children about their own Advent calendars or ones they have seen, drawing out ideas of:

- the number of days on the Advent calendar;
- our feelings of anticipation as we open each door;
- Christmas Day is the last day on the calendar;
- the Advent calendar leads us towards Christmas Day;
- our feelings of anticipation as we think of Christmas Day.

TALKING POINTS

Tell Jesus' words from Luke about his second coming. As you work, talk with the children about the significance of Advent calendars. You could include the following points:

- as we open each window, we look forward to Christmas Day;
- Advent is the time when the church prepares for Christmas;
- at Advent we also remember that Jesus will come again;
- Advent is a time of hope for the future;
- we prepare ourselves for Jesus' second coming.

ACTIVITIES

- Together make a large Advent calendar to be used in church. Cut five windows, one for each Sunday of Advent plus Christmas day. Draw a picture for each window.
- Make small individual Advent calendars for the children to take home. If the shapes are cut out beforehand, the calendars could include 25 windows. If the children completely make their own, there will only be time for five windows. To save time, the pictures could be cut from old cards or wrapping paper.
- Make posters with a message such as: Jesus came on the first Christmas Day. Jesus will come again.
- Write a poem about Jesus' coming.

DISPLAY

- Today's theme is preparing for Christmas.
- Advent calendars prepare us for Christmas Day.
- As we open each door, we look forward to Christmas.
- We look forward to Jesus' second coming.
- Our work today is the Advent calendar.

EXPLORING WITH ADULTS

EXPERIENCE

- What experiences and feelings do you associate with Advent calendars?
- What do you see as the significance of the Advent calendar?
- How does the Advent calendar help to prepare us for Christmas?

GOSPEL

- What does the gospel say about the need to keep on guard?
- How do you interpret the message to keep on guard for today?
- What does this gospel say about how we should keep on guard?

APPLICATION

- How can your church best promote the use of the Advent calendar?
- How can you best use the Advent calendar?
- How can the Advent calendar best be used in liturgy?

CELEBRATING TOGETHER

WELCOMING CHILDREN

At an appropriate point in the service, receive the children's Advent calendars. Explain how the Advent calendar keeps us focused on the expectations of Christmas. Invite a child to display an Advent calendar prominently in church and to open the first window. Other work prepared by the children can be appropriately displayed.

HYMNS AND SONGS

Come and Praise
122 Christmas, Christmas
144 Peace is flowing like a river

Hymns Ancient and Modern New Standard
 26 O come, O come, Emmanuel
180 Thou, whose almighty word

4
CHRISTMAS CARDS

PREPARATION

GOSPEL THEME

Prepare the way (Matthew 3.1–12)

The gospel reading is Matthew's account of how John the Baptist prepared for the ministry of Jesus. John makes good use of the text from the prophet Isaiah, 'Prepare the way of the Lord, make his paths straight'. Matthew's account emphasizes the messages of judgement and of conflict with an unrepentant Jewish nation. There is here a note of urgency in the message.

We can begin to experience the significance of the Bible's teaching on the need to prepare the way for the coming of Jesus by exploring the messages of preparation we wish to include in Christmas cards.

AIMS

- to build on our experiences of Christmas cards;
- to help us understand how messages of preparation can be included in Christmas cards;
- to hear Matthew's note of urgency in the message of John the Baptist.

EXPLORING WITH CHILDREN

STARTING

Bring in a packet of unused Christmas cards, choosing those with a Christian picture and message. Talk with the children about Christmas cards, drawing out ideas of:

- any cards they have received so far;
- a few people they will send cards to;
- the pictures the children most like in the displayed cards;
- the best messages written in the cards;
- the way cards help to prepare us for Christmas.

TALKING POINTS

Tell the story from Matthew of John the Baptist. As you work, talk with the children about the significance of Christmas cards. You could include the following points:

- before Jesus started his work, John the Baptist came;
- John's job was to prepare for Jesus' coming;
- at Christmas we prepare our hearts for Jesus' coming;
- Christmas cards remind us of Jesus' birth;
- it is good to choose cards with that message inside.

ACTIVITIES

- Make Christmas cards, one for each child.
- Work together to make a large card to give to the church from your group. Choose an appropriate message to go inside, one of preparation for Christmas.
- Print Christmas cards. Before the session you will need to prepare printing blocks of Christmas symbols (perhaps cut into potatoes). The children can stamp their designs with coloured paint and plan appropriate messages to go inside.
- Bring in old Christmas cards. Look at the messages inside. Cut out appropriate ones to make a collage preparing for Christmas.

DISPLAY

- Today's theme is preparing the way.
- Christmas cards are a message that Christmas is near.
- John the Baptist gave the message to prepare for Jesus' coming.
- We prepare for Christmas.
- Our work today is about Christmas cards.

EXPLORING WITH ADULTS

EXPERIENCE

- What experiences and feelings do you associate with Christmas cards?
- What messages or texts would you value in Christmas cards?
- How can Christmas cards proclaim the message of Advent?

GOSPEL

- What does this gospel say about John the Baptist?
- How do you interpret this message for today?
- What does this gospel say about the judgement of God?

APPLICATION

- How can your church make best use of Christmas cards?
- What do you want to proclaim through the cards you send?
- How can Christmas cards find a place in the liturgy?

CELEBRATING TOGETHER

WELCOMING CHILDREN

At an appropriate point in the service, display the children's Christmas cards. Invite some of the children to read aloud the message in their cards. Have prepared a large display of old Christmas cards and their messages. Draw attention to the opportunities Christians have to proclaim the gospel through Christmas cards.

HYMNS AND SONGS

Come and Praise
  62 Heavenly father, may thy blessing
  98 You shall go out with joy

Hymns Ancient and Modern New Standard
  30 Hark the glad sound! the Saviour comes
  45 To us a child of royal birth

5
CHRISTMAS POSTERS

PREPARATION

GOSPEL THEME

Prepare the way (Mark 1.1–8)

The gospel reading is Mark's account of how John the Baptist prepared for the ministry of Jesus. John is portrayed as the messenger crying in the wilderness 'Prepare the way of the Lord, make his paths straight'. Mark's account emphasizes the appearance of John dressed like Elijah in the Old Testament. Many expected Elijah to return to prepare the way for God's Messiah. There is here a note of great expectancy in the message.

We can begin to experience the significance of the Bible's teaching on the excitement and expectancy surrounding the coming of God's Messiah by exploring the posters and adverts used to generate excitement in Christmas today.

AIMS

● to build on our experiences of Christmas posters and adverts;

● to help us understand how churches can make good use of Christmas posters;

● to hear Mark's note of expectancy in the message of John the Baptist.

EXPLORING WITH CHILDREN

STARTING

Bring in some Christmas adverts. Look for a variety, perhaps including special Christmas music, Christmas food and toys. Look through these together, drawing out ideas of:

● other Christmas adverts they have seen;

● which adverts excite them most;

● the way they want to respond to these adverts;

● the excitement they feel about Christmas coming;

● any preparations they have made so far for Christmas;

● John the Baptist gave the message to prepare before Jesus began his work.

TALKING POINTS

Tell the story from Mark of John the Baptist. As you work, talk with the children about the significance of Christmas. You could include the following points:

● John the Baptist gave the message that Jesus would come;

● the people were to prepare themselves for Jesus' coming;

● at Christmas we feel excited and full of hope at the thought of our presents;

● we can feel excited and full of hope as we remember Jesus' coming;

● we can choose Christmas messages to share that excitement.

ACTIVITIES

- Make individual Christmas posters or adverts for the children to take home and display. Discuss the message of Christmas to put on these posters.
- Work together to make several large Christmas posters to display in the church.
- Search through papers, magazines and old cards for adverts with Christian messages. Display these in a collage of words and pictures.
- Make a poster of John's message. It could be a long narrow poster to go along a passageway, using the shapes of feet and each word in a different footprint.

DISPLAY

- Today's theme is preparing the way.
- Posters and adverts give the message of Christmas.
- The message of Advent is to prepare.
- Like John the Baptist, we prepare for Jesus' coming.
- Our work today is about Christmas posters.

EXPLORING WITH ADULTS

EXPERIENCE

- Which Christmas posters and adverts do you remember best?
- What do you recall about the churches' Christmas posters?
- How can Christmas posters best proclaim the gospel?

GOSPEL

- What does this gospel say about John the Baptist?

- How do you interpret this message for today?
- What does this gospel say about the expectancy of God's people?

APPLICATION

- How can your church make best use of Christmas posters?
- How can you make best use of Christmas posters?
- What place is there for Christmas posters in liturgy?

CELEBRATING TOGETHER

WELCOMING CHILDREN

At an appropriate point in the service, invite the children to hold up their Christmas posters. Invite some of the children to explain what they chose to show on their posters. Have prepared a large display of Christmas posters and adverts. Draw attention to how the local church can use Christmas posters.

HYMNS AND SONGS

Come and Praise
114 Flick'ring candles in the night
147 Make me a channel of your peace

Hymns Ancient and Modern New Standard
26 O come, O come, Emmanuel
31 Come, thou long-expected Jesus

6
CHRISTMAS DECORATIONS

PREPARATION

GOSPEL THEME

Prepare the way (Luke 3.1–6)

The gospel reading is Luke's account of how John the Baptist prepared for the ministry of Jesus. For Luke, John is no longer portrayed as the returned Elijah, but as the last of the long line of prophets. Now John's message 'Prepare the way of the Lord, make his paths straight' leads straight to the proclamation 'and all flesh shall see the salvation of God'. There is here the note of confidence that the salvation brought by Jesus is for the whole world, not only for the Jewish nation.

We can begin to experience the significance of the Bible's teaching on preparing the way for Jesus to all nations by exploring some of the different traditions associated with Christmas decorations in different parts of the world.

AIMS

- to build on our experiences of Christmas decorations;
- to help us understand how different countries have different forms of Christmas decoration;
- to hear Luke's note of confidence that Christmas is for all peoples.

EXPLORING WITH CHILDREN

STARTING

Bring in a box of Christmas decorations. Look at these with the children, discussing decorations and drawing out ideas of:

- decorations the children have at home;
- decorations the children have seen in the streets;
- decorations the children may have seen in books;
- decorations the children may have seen on overseas holidays;
- the excitement the children feel when they see decorations.

TALKING POINTS

Tell the story from Luke of John the Baptist. As you work, talk with the children about the significance of Christmas. You could include the following points:

- the task of John the Baptist was to prepare for Jesus;
- John's father prophesied about Jesus;
- Jesus would 'give light to those who sit in darkness';
- Jesus' birth was for all people in the world;
- when we celebrate at Christmas we join with people everywhere.

ACTIVITIES

- Make paper chains to decorate the church.
- Make strings of popcorn (an American custom) to take home and decorate your tree.
- Look through encyclopedias or Christmas books for details of Christmas customs in other countries.
- Learn an Advent carol from another country, such as 'Silent Night' which originated in Austria. Make a decorated copy of your chosen carol to display at home.

DISPLAY

- Today's theme is preparing the way.
- Christmas is for all people everywhere.
- We learnt about Christmas decorations in other lands.
- Special decorations help us prepare for Christmas.
- Our work today is about Christmas decorations.

EXPLORING WITH ADULTS

EXPERIENCE

- What are your favourite Christmas decorations and why?
- What do you know about Christmas decorations in other countries?
- How can Christmas decorations symbolize the universal relevance of Christmas?

GOSPEL

- What does this gospel say about John the Baptist's message?
- How do you interpret this message for today?

- What does this gospel say about the universality of Christmas?

APPLICATION

- How can your church make best use of Christmas decorations?
- How can you make best use of Christmas decorations?
- What place is there for Christmas decorations in liturgy?

CELEBRATING TOGETHER

WELCOMING CHILDREN

At an appropriate point in the service, invite the children to set up their Christmas decorations. Invite some of the children to talk about what they have made. Develop the international atmosphere by singing an Advent carol from another country or by telling a story about Christmas customs in another country.

HYMNS AND SONGS

Come and Praise
  49 We are climbing Jesus' ladder, ladder
127 Christmas time is here

Hymns Ancient and Modern New Standard
  45 To us a child of royal birth
166 Lord, thy word abideth

7

WRAPPING PRESENTS

PREPARATION

GOSPEL THEME

John the Baptist (Matthew 11.2–11)

John the Baptist holds a prominent place in the season of Advent, since he is seen as the forerunner who prepares the way for Jesus. In this passage from Matthew, Jesus invites the crowds to reflect on their experiences of John. It is not sufficient simply to be curious about John, we need to penetrate the surface appearances to see what stands behind them. We need to come to a clear view on John's place in God's plans for the people of God.

We can begin to experience the significance of the Bible's teaching on the forerunner by exploring how we prepare for Christmas by preparing Christmas presents. The wrapping is an important part of Christmas presents.

AIMS

- to build on our experiences of Christmas wrappings;
- to help us understand how the wrappings add meaning to what is within;
- to respond to Matthew's challenge to see the significance of John the Baptist.

EXPLORING WITH CHILDREN

STARTING

Bring in some Christmas wrapping paper. Choose contrasting examples so that you show Christian symbols as well as Christmas trees. Discuss the paper, drawing out ideas of:

- any presents the children have wrapped so far;
- how they feel when they see wrapped presents;
- if they prefer presents wrapped or unwrapped;
- the different types of symbols on your paper;
- which best shows the true meaning of Christmas.

TALKING POINTS

Tell Jesus' words from Matthew about John. As you work, talk with the children about the significance of Christmas wrappings. You could include the following points:

- one of the ways we prepare for Christmas is by wrapping presents;
- before a person can see the present, he or she sees the wrapper;
- John the Baptist was like wrapping paper for Jesus;
- before Jesus taught people, John warned that Jesus would come;
- Jesus called John a messenger.

ACTIVITIES

- Make your own wrapping paper. A simple, effective way is to print on sheets of white or brown paper with coloured paint. If you made printing blocks for your Christmas cards, you could use these again for the wrapping paper.

- Prepare a design for wrapping paper to photocopy onto A3 coloured paper. It can contain typed or written messages such as 'Peace at Christmas' as well as simple illustrations by the children. Sell sheets in aid of a chosen charity.

- Write a special message about Jesus. Place it in a box and wrap it with bright paper to give to someone.

- If your church gives presents to children in need, you could spend this time wrapping these gifts.

DISPLAY

- Today's theme is the importance of John the Baptist.
- Jesus called John a messenger.
- Christmas wrappings excite us about the present inside.
- We made wrapping paper to prepare for Christmas.
- Our work today is Christmas wrappings.

EXPLORING WITH ADULTS

EXPERIENCE

- What are your special memories of Christmas wrappings?
- What do the wrappings say to you about the gift or giver?
- How much do you try to look behind the wrappings?

GOSPEL

- What does this gospel reading tell you about the forerunner?
- How do you interpret this message for today?
- What does this gospel say about the need to prepare?

APPLICATION

- How can your church make best use of Christmas wrappings?
- How can you make best use of Christmas wrappings?
- What place is there for Christmas wrappings in liturgy?

CELEBRATING TOGETHER

WELCOMING CHILDREN

At an appropriate point in the service, invite the children to display their Christmas wrappings and to discuss what they have decided to do. Prepare some examples of how Christmas wrappings might be used to remind people of the deep meaning of Christmas.

HYMNS AND SONGS

Come and Praise
26 There is singing in the desert
127 Christmas time is here

Hymns Ancient and Modern New Standard
24 Hark, a thrilling voice is sounding
27 On Jordan's bank the Baptist's cry

8
MAKING PRESENTS

PREPARATION

GOSPEL THEME

John the Baptist (John 1.6–8, 19–28)

John the Baptist holds a prominent place in the season of Advent since he is seen as the forerunner who prepares the way for Jesus. In John's gospel the Baptist is called 'a witness testifying to the light'. John's gospel is keen to emphasize that the Baptist comes only as a forerunner whose job is to direct attention away from himself and toward the one who comes after him.

We can begin to experience the significance of the Bible's teaching on the forerunner by exploring how we prepare for Christmas by preparing Christmas presents. Making Christmas presents is an important part of this tradition.

AIMS

● to build on our experiences of making Christmas presents;

● to help us understand how making presents prepares us for Christmas;

● to grasp how John's gospel sees the Baptist as the forerunner.

EXPLORING WITH CHILDREN

STARTING

Bring in a present that you have made or a home-made present that you have been given. Discuss the present, drawing out ideas of:

● presents that the children have made themselves;

● home-made presents that the children have been given;

● the enjoyment we get from making presents;

● the excitement we feel as we prepare the presents;

● making presents is a way of preparing ourselves for Christmas.

TALKING POINTS

Tell John's account of the work of John the Baptist. As you work, talk with the children about the significance of making Christmas presents. You could include the following points:

● presents can be made at any time before Christmas;

● making presents is part of our preparation for Christmas;

● it helps us realize that Christmas is coming;

● John the Baptist spoke of Jesus coming to God's people;

● John was part of the preparation for Jesus' work.

ACTIVITIES

- Make pot-pourri bags. Use pinking shears to cut out large circles of light material. Place the pot pourri in the centre. Draw up the edges and hold them in place with an elastic band. Tie on a ribbon.
- Cook some Christmas biscuits to give as a present.
- Make gift tags to use or to give away in packs of six. Use pinking shears to cut around old Christmas card pictures. Use the blank back for writing.
- Make calendars as gifts. Glue calendar tabs to sheets of A4 card. Decorate the sheet with a Christmas scene.

DISPLAY

- Today's theme is the work of John the Baptist.
- John the Baptist prepared the way for Jesus' work.
- We make presents to prepare for Christmas.
- Our work today is about making Christmas presents.

EXPLORING WITH ADULTS

EXPERIENCE

- What are your experiences of making Christmas presents?
- What is special about receiving a present someone has made for you?
- How does making presents prepare us for Christmas?

GOSPEL

- What does this gospel reading tell you about the forerunner?

- How do you interpret this message for today?
- What does this gospel say about how we should prepare?

APPLICATION

- How can your church be involved in making Christmas presents?
- How can you be involved in making Christmas presents?
- What place is there for our own Christmas presents in liturgy?

CELEBRATING TOGETHER

WELCOMING CHILDREN

At an appropriate point in the service, invite the children to display the presents which they have made and to talk about why they have made them. Arrange for some members of the congregation to add to the display some Christmas presents which they have made and to talk about them.

HYMNS AND SONGS

Come and Praise
21 Come and praise the Lord our king
59 I will bring to you

Hymns Ancient and Modern New Standard
26 O come, O come, Emmanuel
53 Songs of thankfulness and praise

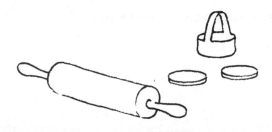

9
GIVING PRESENTS

PREPARATION

GOSPEL THEME

John the Baptist (Luke 3.7–18)

John the Baptist holds a prominent place in the season of Advent since he is seen as the forerunner who prepares the way for Jesus. In Luke's gospel John's message is very much concerned with the quality of life with which his hearers should prepare for the coming of the Messiah. When the crowds asked John 'What then should we do?' his reply was direct. 'Whoever has two coats must share with anyone who has none; and whoever has food must do likewise.'

We can begin to experience the significance of the Bible's teaching on the forerunner by exploring how we give presents at Christmas. At their best, Christmas presents can be a sign of a generous spirit.

AIMS

- to build on our experiences of preparing to give Christmas presents;
- to help us understand how giving presents prepares us for Christmas;
- to grasp John's teaching on sharing our resources.

EXPLORING WITH CHILDREN

STARTING

Bring in a wrapped box containing enough small items (such as sweets, pencils or rubbers) for each child. Pass the present around, encouraging them to shake it and guess the contents. Open it together and share the gifts around. Discuss giving presents, drawing out ideas of:

- how you felt, planning the present;
- how you felt, seeing their enjoyment;
- presents the children have given;
- why we give presents;
- we prepare for Christmas as we plan presents to give.

TALKING POINTS

Tell John the Baptist's words from Luke. As you work, talk with the children about the significance of giving presents. You could include the following points:

- at Christmas we give presents to our friends;
- John the Baptist told people to give whenever they could;
- John told people to get their hearts and lives ready for Jesus;
- he said that people with more than they needed should give to people who do not have enough;
- we can be generous at Christmas and all year round.

ACTIVITIES

- List people to whom you plan to give presents. Make gift tags for these presents.
- Write an acrostic based on the word GIVING. In an acrostic the chosen word is printed down the page so that each line begins with a letter of that word.
- Create a dance or a drama about giving. You could start with a pile of boxes in the centre of a circle of children. The children could frantically grab for the boxes, getting more and more unhappy. Pause for a moment of silence and then look around and start giving boxes to others.
- Decorate small boxes. Cut a slit in the top suitable for coins. Use these for collecting small change at home, to give to those in need at Christmas.

DISPLAY

- Today's theme is giving presents.
- John the Baptist said to give generously.
- We can give to others all year round.
- John the Baptist prepared people for Jesus.
- Our work today is about giving presents.

EXPLORING WITH ADULTS

EXPERIENCE

- What are your experiences of giving Christmas presents?
- What is special about giving Christmas presents?
- How does giving presents prepare us for Christmas?

GOSPEL

- What does this gospel reading tell you about the message of the forerunner?
- How do you interpret this message for today?
- What does this gospel say about how we should give?

APPLICATION

- How should your church be involved in giving Christmas presents?
- How should you give Christmas presents?
- What place is there for Christmas presents in liturgy?

CELEBRATING TOGETHER

WELCOMING CHILDREN

At an appropriate point in the service, invite the children to display their work on giving presents and to talk about the display. Have some mystery parcels ready wrapped and invite the children to guess what is inside.

HYMNS AND SONGS

Come and Praise
  29 From the darkness came light
  64 The wise may bring their learning

Hymns Ancient and Modern New Standard
  24 Hark, a thrilling voice is sounding
  27 On Jordan's bank the Baptist's cry

10
THE MANGER

PREPARATION

GOSPEL THEME

Mary (Matthew 1.18–25)

On the last Sunday of Advent the church focuses attention on Mary, who prepared for the first Christmas in a very special way. According to the traditions of both Matthew and Luke, Mary was with child from the Holy Spirit. The gospel reading from Matthew explores the conception from Joseph's perspective and draws on the authority of the Old Testament prophecy 'Look, the virgin shall conceive and bear a son, and they shall name him Emmanuel'.

We can begin to share in Mary's experience by making our own preparations for the birth of Jesus. According to the tradition, part of this preparation involves setting out the manger in which the baby was cradled.

AIMS

● to build on our experiences of preparing a manger for the nativity;

● to help us understand that Jesus was born as any other human baby;

● to grasp the central role of Mary in the nativity.

EXPLORING WITH CHILDREN

STARTING

Bring in some baby items such as a pram or a carry cot. Ask the children about baby siblings or cousins or neighbours. Talk about where these babies sleep, drawing out ideas of:

● the care with which parents prepare the cot or pram;

● the number of sleeping places the baby might have;

● the covers in the cot or pram or carry cot;

● other items that could be used in an emergency, such as a drawer or toy basket;

● Jesus was put to sleep in an animals' feed box.

TALKING POINTS

Tell today's part of the Christmas story from Matthew. Let the children tell you about the birth of Jesus. As you work, talk with the children about Mary and the manger. You could include the following points:

● Mary is special because she was chosen to be the mother of Jesus;

● Mary agreed to have the baby;

● Mary must have taken the baby's wrappings with her, ready to use;

● Joseph and Mary had no cradle, so they used what was near;

● the manger was a safe place in the stable.

ACTIVITIES

- If your church has a special manger for display each year, the children could help to put in the straw and get it ready. If you do not have one then make one.
- Make individual mangers for the children to take home for their own nativity scenes. Cut down cereal or grocery boxes. Paint them or cover them with paper. Fill them with straw or hay. Make figures for Mary and Joseph from cut-down cardboard tubes covered with material for clothes and a ball of paper or cotton wool for a head.
- Plan and record an interview with 'Mary' about the baby's birth.
- Prepare a display of modern baby sleep items and the type that Jesus used.

DISPLAY

- Today's theme is Mary.
- Mary prepared for Jesus' birth.
- Jesus slept in a manger.
- We made mangers to take home.
- Our work today is about the manger.

EXPLORING WITH ADULTS

EXPERIENCE

- What are your experiences of seeing a manger at Christmas?
- What messages does the Christmas manger convey to you?
- How does preparing a manger focus our thoughts on the nativity?

GOSPEL

- What does the gospel reading tell you about Mary?

- How do you interpret this message for today?
- What does the angel's message say about the person of Jesus?

APPLICATION

- How should the church present the manger today?
- How should you use the image of the manger today?
- What place is there for the manger in liturgy?

CELEBRATING TOGETHER

WELCOMING CHILDREN

At an appropriate point in the service, invite the children to bring in their manger and to display it in church ready for the Christmas services. Arrange for the manger to be complemented by a display of prams, cradles and cots.

HYMNS AND SONGS

Come and Praise
21 Come and praise the Lord our king
23 Jesus, good above all other

Hymns Ancient and Modern New Standard
33 Of the father's love begotten
42 In the bleak midwinter

11
THE STABLE

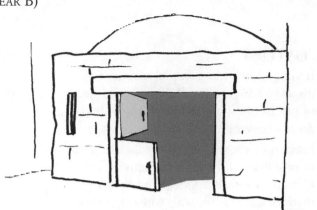

PREPARATION

GOSPEL THEME

Mary (Luke 1.26–38)

On the last Sunday of Advent the church focuses attention on Mary, who prepared for the first Christmas in a very special way. According to the traditions of both Matthew and Luke, Mary was with child from the Holy Spirit. The gospel reading for Luke explores the conception from Mary's perspective. The news is brought to Mary by the angel Gabriel.

We can begin to share in Mary's experience by making our own preparations for the birth of Jesus. According to the tradition, part of this preparation involves building the stable in which the baby was born.

AIMS

● to build on our images of the stable at Bethlehem;

● to help us understand that Jesus was born as a human baby;

● to grasp the central role of Mary in the nativity.

EXPLORING WITH CHILDREN

STARTING

Bring in a picture or photograph of a modern hospital. Ask the children if they have ever visited a hospital to see a new-born baby. Talk about the birth of a baby, drawing out ideas of:

● most babies in this country are born in a hospital;

● hospitals the children have visited;

● hospitals are kept as clean as possible;

● doctors and nurses are there to help if needed;

● Jesus was born in a stable, an animal shelter.

TALKING POINTS

Tell today's part of the Christmas story from Luke. Let the children tell you about the birth of Jesus. As you work, talk with the children about Mary and the stable. You could include the following points:

● Mary is special because she was chosen to be the mother of Jesus;

● Mary agreed to have the baby;

● Joseph and Mary had no hospital but they looked for a safe place;

● the stable was probably cosy and quiet;

● Mary loved her baby and cared for him as well as she could.

ACTIVITIES

- If your church has a special stable put out for display each year, the children could help to get it ready and assemble it. If you do not have one, then work together to make a stable from a large grocery box. Make figures for Mary and Joseph from cut-down cardboard tubes (such as clingfilm tubes) covered with material for clothes and a ball of paper or cotton wool for a head.
- Make individual stables for the children to take home for their own nativity scenes. Use grocery boxes from your local super-market. Cut off the flaps. Paint them or cover them with paper. Glue straw or hay on the floor. Add Mary and Joseph and a small box for a manger.
- Find or make simple props to dress up as animals for the stable.
- Write an article for the 'Bethlehem Times' about the baby born in the stable. You could include an advert for the stable from the owner!

DISPLAY

- Today's theme is Mary.
- Mary prepared for the birth of Jesus.
- Jesus was born in a stable.
- We made stables to take home.
- Our work today is about the stable.

EXPLORING WITH ADULTS

EXPERIENCE

- What are your images of the place in which Jesus was born?
- What messages does the Christmas stable convey to you?
- How does preparing the stable focus our thoughts on the nativity?

GOSPEL

- What does this gospel reading tell you about Mary?
- How do you interpret this message for today?
- What does the angel's message say about the person of Jesus?

APPLICATION

- How should the church present the Christmas stable today?
- How should you use the image of the Christmas stable today?
- What place is there for the stable in liturgy?

CELEBRATING TOGETHER

WELCOMING CHILDREN

At an appropriate point in the service, invite the children to set up their stable in church ready for the Christmas services. Some children might like to dress up as animals within the stable.

HYMNS AND SONGS

Come and Praise
123 Mary had a baby, yes, Lord
127 Christmas time is here

Hymns Ancient and Modern New Standard
40 O little town of Bethlehem
46 Once in royal David's city

12
THE BABY

GOSPEL THEME

Mary (Luke 1.39–55)

On the last Sunday of Advent the church focuses attention on Mary, who prepared for the first Christmas in a very special way. According to Luke, Mary the mother of Jesus and Elizabeth the mother of John the Baptist were relatives and were pregnant at the same time. In this gospel passage the two pregnant women meet and Elizabeth acknowledges the supremacy of Mary's unborn child.

We can begin to share in Mary's experience by making our own preparations for the birth of Jesus. Behind the piety of nativity is the central truth of the Christian faith that Jesus was born a baby who needed clothing, feeding and caring like all other babies.

AIMS

- to build on our experiences of preparing for a new baby;
- to help us understand that Jesus was born as a human baby;
- to grasp the central role of Mary in the nativity.

STARTING

Bring in a selection of baby clothes (and even a baby if you know some willing parents). Talk about these together, drawing out ideas of:

- babies the children know;
- clothes that a baby wears;
- other things that a baby needs;
- things that we buy for a baby and those that we make;
- the preparation that parents make before a baby is born.

TALKING POINTS

Tell today's part of the Christmas story from Luke. Let the children tell you about the birth of Jesus. As you work, talk with the children about Mary and the birth of the baby. You could include the following points:

- Mary is special because she was chosen to be the mother of Jesus;
- her cousin Elizabeth had a baby just before her;
- Elizabeth's baby grew up to be John the Baptist;
- Mary prepared for her baby just as mothers today prepare;
- Jesus was just like any other baby.

ACTIVITIES

- Make models of the baby in the manger to take home. Use cardboard boxes for the mangers. Place hay inside. Prepare 'babies' ready to place inside on Christmas day. These could be polystyrene balls attached to cardboard cylinders wrapped in fabric.
- If you have a new-born baby in the church, or if a baby is expected soon, prepare a welcome basket with a few simple baby needs plus cards from the children.
- Prepare a picture display of things a baby needs.
- Paint a large wall mural of the stable, featuring the manger ready for the baby.

DISPLAY

- Today's theme is Mary.
- Mary prepared for her baby's birth.
- Jesus was born as a human baby.
- We learnt about the things a baby needs.
- Our work today is about the baby.

EXPLORING WITH ADULTS

EXPERIENCE

- What are your images of the newly born Jesus?
- What messages are conveyed to you by a baby?
- How does thinking about a baby focus our thoughts on the nativity?

GOSPEL

- What does this gospel reading tell you about Mary?

- How do you interpret this message for today?
- What does Elizabeth's exclamation say about the person of Jesus?

APPLICATION

- How should the church present the image of Jesus the baby today?
- How should you use the image of Jesus the baby today?
- What place is there for the image of Jesus the baby in liturgy?

CELEBRATING TOGETHER

WELCOMING CHILDREN

At an appropriate point in the service, invite the children to display what they have prepared to welcome the new-born baby. Invite some of the children to talk about what they have prepared.

HYMNS AND SONGS

Come and Praise
- 24 Go, tell it on the mountain
- 121 The Virgin Mary had a baby boy

Hymns Ancient and Modern New Standard
- 31 Come, thou long-expected Jesus
- 43 A great and mighty wonder

Introduction to Christmas and Epiphany

Both the church and the secular world remain conscious of the twelve days of Christmas between Christmas day and the feast of the Epiphany. This twelve-day period within the church's calendar provides opportunities to explore the nativity and Epiphany narratives within the gospels.

Often, however, these important narratives are not used to best effect on the Sundays within this twelve-day period, when the children of the church may have the best opportunities to explore these stories and to share them with the adult members of the congregation. For this reason, we have chosen to develop the gospel lections appointed for Christmas Day and for the feast of the Epiphany as alternatives to the gospel readings appointed for the first and for the second Sundays after Christmas.

The lectionary suggests three gospel passages for Christmas Day. The two passages suggested from Luke's gospel focus on the shepherds and on the angelic chorus. The passage suggested from John's gospel is the prologue.

The gospel passages suggested by the lectionary for the first Sunday after Christmas (which we have chosen not to use) explore the first twelve years of Jesus' life, by focusing on the flight into Egypt and return to Nazareth, on the encounter with Simeon and Anna in the temple, and on the boy Jesus being found in the temple talking with the teachers. Young children may be surprised to encounter these narratives so quickly after Christmas Day and before the feast of the Epiphany.

While only one gospel passage is suggested for the feast of the Epiphany, this is a rich narrative which can be explored from several different angles.

13
THE SHEPHERDS

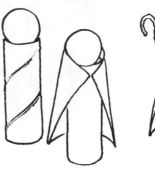

PREPARATION

GOSPEL THEME

Nativity (Luke 2.1–14)

Luke's account of the nativity gives prominence to the shepherds. The birth of Jesus went neither unnoticed nor uncelebrated, because the shepherds were there to pay homage. In the Christmas tradition the shepherds have come to represent the ordinary people of first-century Palestine, the people whose lives the Saviour was born to change.

We can begin to share in the mystery of the holy nativity by putting ourselves in the shepherds' shoes and by travelling with them to Bethlehem, as if for the first time. The Christmas nativity scene in church can be left devoid of shepherds until they arrive in place on the first Sunday after Christmas.

AIMS

- to build on our images of the Christmas shepherds;
- to share in the shepherds' pilgrimage to Bethlehem;
- to offer worship to the newborn Christ.

EXPLORING WITH CHILDREN

STARTING

Bring in pictures of sheep and shepherds. Discuss sheep and the care a shepherd has for the flock, both in modern times and in Bible times, drawing out ideas of:

- the importance of sheep;
- the need for sheep's wool in Bible times;
- the work of a shepherd providing food for the sheep;
- the work of a shepherd providing protection;
- shepherds in Bible times were very ordinary people.

TALKING POINTS

Tell today's part of the Christmas story from Luke. As you work, talk with the children about the significance of the shepherds. You could include the following points:

- the shepherds were ordinary people;
- God chose to give them the message of the Messiah's birth;
- the Messiah had been promised for many years;
- the shepherds were willing to go to Bethlehem to see;
- they praised God.

ACTIVITIES

- If your church has a special nativity scene for display each year, the children could help to assemble the shepherds and get them ready. If you do not have one, then work together to make one.
- Make figures of shepherds for the children to take home for their own nativity scenes. Use cut-down cardboard tubes (such as clingfilm tubes) covered with material for clothes and a ball of paper or cotton wool for a head.
- Plan and record an interview with 'Mary' about the visit of the shepherds.
- Prepare costumes for the children to dress up as shepherds visiting the stable. Talk with them about how they might feel and what they might do.

DISPLAY

- Today's theme is the nativity.
- The message of Jesus' birth was given to ordinary people.
- The shepherds visited the baby Jesus.
- The shepherds praised God.
- Our work today is about the shepherds.

EXPLORING WITH ADULTS

EXPERIENCE

- What are your images of the Christmas shepherds?
- What messages are conveyed to you by the shepherds?
- How does thinking about the shepherds focus your thoughts on the nativity?

GOSPEL

- What does the gospel reading tell you about the nativity?
- How do you interpret this message for today?
- What does the passage say about the person of Jesus?

APPLICATION

- How should the church present the tradition of the shepherds today?
- How should you use the image of the shepherds today?
- What place is there for the image of the shepherds in liturgy?

CELEBRATING TOGETHER

WELCOMING CHILDREN

At an appropriate point in the service, invite the children to bring their shepherds to the Christmas nativity scene. If the children have prepared shepherd costumes, invite them to cluster round the manger and to sing an appropriate carol.

HYMNS AND SONGS

Come and Praise
116 There's a star in the east on Christmas morn
121 The Virgin Mary had a baby boy

Hymns Ancient and Modern New Standard
37 While shepherds watched their flocks by night
44 Behold, the great creator makes

14
THE ANGELS

PREPARATION

GOSPEL THEME

Nativity (Luke 2.8–20)

Luke's account of the nativity gives prominence not only to the shepherds, but to the angels as well. The birth of Jesus was heralded and celebrated not only by the world of humans, but by the world of angels as well. According to Luke, a multitude of the heavenly host praised God, saying 'Glory to God in the highest heaven, and on earth peace among those whom he favours!'

We can begin to share in the mystery of the holy nativity by putting ourselves in the presence of the heavenly host and by joining in their hymn of praise. The Christmas nativity scene can be left devoid of angels until they arrive in place on the first Sunday after Christmas.

AIMS

● to build on our images of the Christmas angels;
● to join in the angels' hymn of praise;
● to offer worship to the newborn Christ.

EXPLORING WITH CHILDREN

STARTING

Bring in some pictures or Christmas cards depicting angels. Discuss these with the children, drawing out ideas of:

● other pictures or paintings of angels they have seen;
● carvings or stained glass windows of angels;
● information about angels that they know;
● a reminder of the angel who visited Mary and Joseph;
● an angel announced Jesus' birth to ordinary people nearby.

TALKING POINTS

Tell today's part of the Christmas story from Luke. As you work, talk with the children about the significance of the angels. You could include the following points:

● angels are messengers sent from God;
● one angel gave the shepherds the message of Jesus' birth;
● many angels praised God;
● because of the angels, the shepherds visited Jesus;
● we can still worship Jesus today.

ACTIVITIES

- If your church has a special nativity scene displayed each year, the children could help to prepare the angels. If you do not have one but have been working on one over the past weeks, then make angel figures now.
- Make Christmas angels out of lace paper doilies. Cut out a triangular section of about one-third. Fold the larger section to form a cone and staple or glue it together. Fold the smaller section in half and round out the top (heart shape) to make wings. Attach these to the back of the cone. Add a cotton-wool ball for the head.
- Make angel costumes for the children to wear. Use old sheets decorated with tinsel.
- Compose some angelic music using various instruments.

DISPLAY

- Today's theme is the nativity.
- The angels gave God's message to the shepherds.
- The angels worshipped God.
- We can worship Jesus today.
- Our work today is about angels.

EXPLORING WITH ADULTS

EXPERIENCE

- What are your images of the Christmas angels?
- What messages are conveyed to you by the angels?
- How does thinking about the angels focus your thoughts on the nativity?

GOSPEL

- What does the gospel reading tell you about the nativity?
- How do you interpret this message for today?
- What does this passage say about the person of Jesus?

APPLICATION

- How should the church present the tradition of the angels today?
- How should you use the image of the angels today?
- What place is there for the image of the angels in liturgy?

CELEBRATING TOGETHER

WELCOMING CHILDREN

At an appropriate point in the service, invite the children to bring their angels to the Christmas nativity scene. If the children have prepared angel costumes, invite them to cluster round the stable and to sing an appropriate carol.

HYMNS AND SONGS

Come and Praise
117 I want to see your baby boy
121 The Virgin Mary had a baby boy

Hymns Ancient and Modern New Standard
 35 Hark, the herald-angels sing
 39 Angels, from the realms of glory

15
CHRISTMAS LIGHTS

PREPARATION

GOSPEL THEME

Nativity (John 1.1–14)

The prologue to John's gospel sets out the mystery of the incarnation: 'the Word became flesh and lived among us'. In this prologue the incarnate Word is described as 'the light of all people'. This light 'shines in the darkness, and the darkness did not overcome it'. Then later in his gospel John develops the theme of Jesus as the Light of the World.

We can begin to grasp the significance of John's powerful image of Jesus as the Light by exploring our own experiences of the lights of Christmas.

AIMS

- to build on our experiences of the lights of Christmas;
- to see Jesus as the light of the people;
- to offer worship to the word made flesh.

EXPLORING WITH CHILDREN

STARTING

Bring in Christmas tree lights or candles or pictures of Christmas street lights. Discuss these, drawing out ideas of:

- street lights the children have seen;
- the lights they have around their house at Christmas;
- any special Christmas lights in the church;
- the beauty of the lights in a dark evening;
- Jesus is known as the light of all people.

TALKING POINTS

Tell John's description of Jesus. As you work, talk with the children about the significance of light. You could include the following points:

- the Bible describes Jesus as 'the light of all people';
- light shines out clearly in the darkness;
- Jesus' life shone clearly to those who met him;
- the darkness could not overcome Jesus;
- Jesus' life and teaching still shine for us today.

ACTIVITIES

- Decorate candles with soft coloured wax, available at art supply shops. This can be shaped by hand and pressed onto candles.
- Make Christmas candleholders. Fill small garden pots with soil or sand. Plant the candle inside firmly and decorate with holly.
- Cut 'windows' in the sides and sloping top of cardboard milk cartons. Cover the side windows with Cellophane but leave the top ones. Attach a candle inside with lots of Plasticine (which will also weight it down). Staple the top together and add a handle. Light the candle through the top windows with a taper.
- Make and decorate cardboard frames to fit around light switches. Write on them 'Jesus is the light of the world'.

DISPLAY

- Today's theme is the nativity.
- Jesus is a light to all people.
- Christmas lights shine out in the darkness.
- We worship Jesus, the light of the world.
- Our work today is about Christmas lights.

EXPLORING WITH ADULTS

EXPERIENCE

- What are your experiences of Christmas lights?
- What messages are conveyed to you by Christmas lights?
- How does thinking about Christmas lights focus your thoughts on the nativity?

GOSPEL

- What does the gospel reading tell you about the image of light?
- How do you interpret this message for today?
- What does the prologue to John's gospel say about the person of Jesus?

APPLICATION

- How should the church present the image of Jesus as Light today?
- How should you use the image of Jesus as Light today?
- What place is there for the image of Jesus as Light in liturgy?

CELEBRATING TOGETHER

WELCOMING CHILDREN

At an appropriate point in the service, invite the children to bring their lights to the Christmas nativity scene. If they have made or decorated candles, arrange for these to be lit and the church lights dimmed while an appropriate carol is sung.

HYMNS AND SONGS

Come and Praise
114 Flick'ring candles in the night
118 When the winter day is dying

Hymns Ancient and Modern New Standard
36 Christians, awake! salute the happy morn
41 It came upon the midnight clear

16
CHRISTMAS STAR

PREPARATION

GOSPEL THEME

Epiphany (Matthew 2.1–12)

Matthew's gospel completes the Christmas story with the tradition of the visitors from the East. This is a rich tradition which contains many important images. One of these images is the Christmas star. According to this image, the wise men from the East seem to have been astrologers who were led to the infant Jesus by following the star. The star stopped over the place where the child Jesus was living.

We can begin to grasp the significance of Matthew's powerful image of the Christmas star by exploring our own experiences of stars and the great attraction of the Bethlehem star. The Christmas nativity scene can be left devoid of the star until it is put in place on the Sunday next to Epiphany.

AIMS

● to build on our experiences of stars;
● to follow the Bethlehem star to find Jesus;
● to offer worship to Jesus alongside the wise men.

EXPLORING WITH CHILDREN

STARTING

Bring in a Christmas tree star. Discuss it with the children, drawing out ideas of:

● stars they have seen this Christmas;
● places the stars have been displayed;
● stars on Christmas cards;
● stars they have made at school or at home;
● the star is a Christmas symbol.

TALKING POINTS

Tell today's part of the Christmas story from Matthew. As you work, talk with the children about the significance of the star. You could include the following points:

● the wise men learnt of Jesus' birth from the star;
● because of the star they came to worship him;
● they followed the star to the stable;
● they worshipped Jesus and gave him gifts;
● we can worship Jesus today.

ACTIVITIES

- If your church has a special nativity scene for display each year, the children could prepare the star ready for display. If you have been making a scene for the church, make the star today.
- Make individual stars for the children's own nativity scene at home. Cover cardboard with silver paper. Add glitter.
- Bake biscuits in the shape of stars. Prepare the mixture beforehand. Bake the biscuits while the children return to church. These biscuits can either be taken home or served with morning tea at church.
- Plan and record an interview with 'Mary' about the visit of the wise men.

DISPLAY

- Today's theme is the Epiphany.
- The wise men followed the star to find Jesus.
- The Christmas star leads us to Jesus.
- Like the wise men, we worship Jesus.
- Our work today is about the star.

EXPLORING WITH ADULTS

EXPERIENCE

- What are your experiences of stars?
- What messages are conveyed to you by the stars?
- How does the Christmas star influence your faith?

GOSPEL

- What does the gospel reading tell you about the Bethlehem star?

- How do you interpret this message for today?
- What does the Bethlehem star say about the person of Jesus?

APPLICATION

- How should the church present the Bethlehem star today?
- How should you use the image of the Bethlehem star today?
- What place is there for the Bethlehem star in liturgy?

CELEBRATING TOGETHER

WELCOMING CHILDREN

At an appropriate point in the service, invite the children to present their work on the Bethlehem star. If they have produced a large star, this can be placed over the stable while an appropriate carol is sung.

HYMNS AND SONGS

Come and Praise
120 As I went riding by
126 Little star stay with us

Hymns Ancient and Modern New Standard
48 Earth has many a noble city
49 O worship the Lord in the beauty of holiness

17
CHRISTMAS JOURNEY

PREPARATION

GOSPEL THEME

Epiphany (Matthew 2.1–12)

Matthew's gospel completes the Christmas story with the tradition of the visitors from the East. This is a rich tradition which contains many important images. One of these images is the Christmas journey. According to the tradition, the wise men undertook a long and arduous journey in order to find the infant Christ. The journey brought them face to face with King Herod and with the chief priests and scribes of the people.

We can begin to grasp the significance of Matthew's powerful image of the Christmas journey by exploring our own experiences of journeys and the great attraction of pilgrimage.

AIMS

- to build on our experiences of journeys;
- to join the wise men's journey to find Jesus;
- to offer worship to Jesus alongside the wise men.

EXPLORING WITH CHILDREN

STARTING

Bring in a variety of maps: a street directory, a more general road map, an atlas of the United Kingdom and an atlas of the world. Discuss with the children journeys they have been on, drawing out ideas of:

- places they have been;
- where these places are on the maps;
- why they went on a journey;
- how they travelled;
- people they visited or met on their journey.

TALKING POINTS

Tell today's part of the Christmas story from Matthew. As you work, talk with the children about the significance of the wise men's journey. You could include the following points:

- the wise men travelled a long way;
- they came to Bethlehem from the East (look on a map);
- the purpose of their journey was to see Jesus;
- we do not know how they travelled;
- when they arrived they worshipped Jesus.

ACTIVITIES

- If your church has a special nativity scene put out for display each year, the children could help to get the wise men ready. If you do not have one already but are working on one, make figures for the wise men.
- If you have made individual nativity scenes for home, make figures of the wise men.
- Prepare a dance or mime on the theme of journeys. It could involve packing, putting on journey clothes and travelling from one place to another.
- Prepare clothes in order to dress up as wise men yourselves.

DISPLAY

- Today's theme is the Epiphany.
- The wise men journeyed to see Christ.
- We journey to church to worship Jesus.
- We made figures of the wise men.
- Our work today is about journeys.

EXPLORING WITH ADULTS

EXPERIENCE

- What are your experiences of pilgrimages or special journeys?
- What does the idea of pilgrimage mean to you?
- Is there a place for pilgrimage in your faith?

GOSPEL

- What does the gospel reading tell you about pilgrimage?
- How do you interpret this message for today?

- What does the journey of the wise men say about the person of Jesus?

APPLICATION

- How should the church present pilgrimage today?
- How should you use pilgrimage today?
- What place is there for pilgrimage in liturgy?

CELEBRATING TOGETHER

WELCOMING CHILDREN

At an appropriate point in the service, invite the children to present their work on journeys. If they have made costumes for the journey of the wise men, invite them to process to the stable while an appropriate carol is sung.

HYMNS AND SONGS

Come and Praise
120 As I went riding by
124 Riding out across the desert

Hymns Ancient and Modern New Standard
 50 The heavenly child in stature grows
 51 As with gladness men of old

18 CHRISTMAS GIFTS

PREPARATION

GOSPEL THEME

Epiphany (Matthew 2.1–12)

Matthew's gospel completes the Christmas story with the tradition of the visitors from the East. This is a rich tradition which contains many important images. One of these images is the Christmas gifts. According to the tradition the wise men brought three gifts to the infant Jesus. Each of these gifts is associated tradition-ally with a special meaning. The gift of gold speaks of Jesus' kingship. The gift of frankin-cense speaks of Jesus' priesthood. The gift of myrrh speaks of Jesus' death.

We can begin to grasp the significance of Matthew's powerful image of the Christmas gifts by exploring our own experiences of Christmas gifts and the great attraction of the gold, frankincense and myrrh.

AIMS

- to build on our experiences of Christmas gifts;
- to appreciate the meaning of the gifts of the wise men;
- to offer our gifts to Jesus alongside the wise men.

EXPLORING WITH CHILDREN

STARTING

Bring in a wrapped box. Explain that this box is empty but that you want to think about Christmas gifts. Discuss these with the children drawing out ideas of:

- gifts they gave;
- the reason they chose to buy one particular gift;
- gifts they received;
- the reason people chose such gifts for them;
- often we choose gifts with care.

TALKING POINTS

Tell today's part of the Christmas story from Matthew. As you work, talk with the children about the significance of the wise men's gifts. You could include the following points:

- all three gifts have meanings;
- the gift of gold reminds us that Jesus is king;
- the gift of frankincense reminds us that Jesus is a priest;
- the gift of myrrh reminds us of Jesus' death;
- we can give gifts of our love and our service.

ACTIVITIES

- Prepare articles to symbolize the meaning of the three gifts. These could be a gold crown, a priest's stole and a cross.
- Bring in some plain biscuits and an icing kit. Let the children draw symbols on the biscuits with icing.
- Prepare a colourfully decorated box. Inside it place pieces of paper on which the children can write a sentence of love for Jesus or a promise of service. Emphasize that these gifts will be kept private and will be destroyed after the service without you reading them, unless the children choose to show you first.
- Dress up to present a tableau of the wise men offering their gifts to Jesus.

DISPLAY

- Today's theme is the Epiphany.
- The wise men gave gifts to Jesus.
- The wise men chose gold, frankincense and myrrh.
- We offer our gifts of love and service.
- Our work today is about Christmas gifts.

EXPLORING WITH ADULTS

EXPERIENCE

- What are your experiences of Christmas gifts?
- What messages are conveyed to you by Christmas gifts?

- How do Christmas gifts carry symbolic meaning today?

GOSPEL

- What does the gospel reading tell you about the gifts of the wise men?
- How do you interpret this message for today?
- What do the three gifts say about the person of Jesus?

APPLICATION

- How should the church proclaim the gifts of the wise men today?
- How should the gifts of the wise men influence your life today?
- What place is there for the gifts of the wise men in liturgy?

CELEBRATING TOGETHER

WELCOMING CHILDREN

At an appropriate point in the service, invite the children to present their work on Christmas gifts. If they have produced gifts representing gold, frankincense and myrrh, these can be presented to the baby Jesus while an appropriate carol is sung.

HYMNS AND SONGS

Come and Praise
  59 I will bring to you
117 I want to see your baby boy

Hymns Ancient and Modern New Standard
  47 Brightest and best of the sons of the morning
  52 The people that in darkness sat

Introduction to the Season of Epiphany

The Greek root of the word 'Epiphany' means 'to bring to light' or 'to reveal'. The season of Epiphany begins when the infant Christ is revealed to the wise men from the East. In a sense, the Sundays after Epiphany and before Lent continue this theme.

Because the date of Easter is fixed by the phases of the moon and therefore varies from year to year, the number of Sundays between the feast of Epiphany and the beginning of Lent also varies. The lectionary deals with this by following the first, second, third and fourth Sundays of Epiphany with Sundays counted before Lent. When Easter is early, fewer of the Sundays before Lent are used than when Easter is late.

The way in which the Sundays are numbered and named in this section follows the use of the Church of England and the Church in Wales. Other churches using the Revised Common Lectionary may relate Proper 1 to the Sixth Sunday after Epiphany, and so on.

In all three years, the first Sunday of Epiphany celebrates the baptism of Jesus, when the divine revelation addressed Jesus with the words (Mark 1.11) 'You are my Son, the Beloved; with you I am well pleased'. In all three years, the last Sunday before Lent celebrates the transfiguration, when the divine revelation once again addressed Jesus in similar words (Mark 9.7), 'This is my Son, the Beloved; listen to him!'

In all three years, the second Sunday of Epiphany draws on themes of revelation from John's gospel: Andrew's testimony that 'we have found the Messiah'; Nathanael's affirmation, 'you are the Son of God'; and the wedding at Cana where Jesus performed the first of his signs and revealed his glory.

In year A the Sundays between the third Sunday of Epiphany and the Sunday before Lent draw on the opening chapters of Matthew. The call of the first disciples is followed by five extracts from the Sermon on the Mount.

In year B the Sundays between the third Sunday of Epiphany and the Sunday before Lent draw on the opening chapters of Mark. The call of the first four disciples is followed by four accounts of healing and then by the call of Levi.

In year C the Sundays between the third Sunday of Epiphany and the Sunday before Lent draw on the opening chapters of Luke. Luke's cycle of readings begins with Jesus teaching in the synagogue of Nazareth. This is followed by Jesus' rejection at Nazareth, by the great catch of fish and by three extracts from the Sermon on the Plain.

19 WATER

PREPARATION

GOSPEL THEME

Jesus' baptism (Matthew 3.13–17)

The gospel reading is Matthew's account of the baptism of Jesus. Matthew's account differs from the account in Mark and Luke by presenting the conversation between John and Jesus. The baptism which John offered to the crowds was an outward sign of repentance and cleansing. The baptism which John offered to Jesus, however, was the outward sign of God's anointing. The words 'This is my son' echo Psalm 2, a psalm used to celebrate the anointing of a king.

We can begin to grasp the significance of John the Baptist's powerful image of water as a sign of repentance and cleansing by exploring our own experiences of the cleansing and life-giving power of water.

AIMS

- to build on our experiences of water;
- to appreciate the symbolic power of water;
- to see the baptism by John as a sign of repentance and cleansing.

EXPLORING WITH CHILDREN

STARTING

Bring in some dirty dishes or dirty cloths. Talk about how they could be cleaned, drawing out ideas of:

- rubbing the dishes with a cloth;
- wiping the dishes with sand or dirt;
- wiping the dishes with our hands;
- using liquid soap (no water) on dishes or cloths;
- water as the best way of cleaning.

TALKING POINTS

Tell the story from Matthew of Jesus' baptism. As you work, talk with the children about the significance of this baptism. You could include the following points:

- water makes us clean;
- baptism in water is a sign of being made clean from wrongdoing;
- Jesus had done no wrong;
- he asked John to baptize him;
- this baptism gave the sign that he was God's son.

ACTIVITIES

- Conduct some experiments on dirty rags. Try to get some clean without water. Try others with water. See how important water is for cleansing.
- Make posters about water. Include pictures of all the ways we use water in our homes.
- Write a poem about a time you were very dirty, how you became dirty and how you cleaned yourself.
- Become involved in a very messy activity such as finger painting or clay modelling. First try cleaning your hands with paper towels, then with just soap, then add water.

DISPLAY

- Today's theme is Jesus' baptism.
- Baptism is a sign of cleansing.
- Jesus was baptized in water.
- We need water to clean ourselves.
- Our work today is about water.

EXPLORING WITH ADULTS

EXPERIENCE

- What are your experiences of water?
- What is the symbolic power of water?
- What does water proclaim in baptism?

GOSPEL

- What does the gospel reading tell us about Matthew's understanding of Jesus' baptism?
- How do you interpret this message for today?
- What does the voice say about the person of Jesus?

APPLICATION

- How should the church proclaim baptism today?
- What does baptism mean to you?
- How should baptism be conducted today?

CELEBRATING TOGETHER

WELCOMING CHILDREN

At an appropriate point in the service, invite the children to present their work on water. Invite them to bring water to the font and to fill it ready for baptism.

HYMNS AND SONGS

Come and Praise
  2 Have you heard the raindrops
  7 All creatures of our God and King

Hymns Ancient and Modern New Standard
  442 Christ, when for us you were baptized
  444 Christians, lift up your hearts

20 CORONATION

PREPARATION

GOSPEL THEME

Jesus' baptism (Mark 1.4–11)

The gospel reading is Mark's account of the baptism of Jesus. In this account, Mark presents John dressed like Elijah in the Old Testament. Dressed like this, John's task is to anoint Jesus as God's Messiah. The Hebrew word 'Messiah' means the 'anointed one', 'the King'. John's baptism is confirmed by 'the Spirit descending like a dove' and by the divine voice. The words 'You are my son' echo Psalm 2, a psalm used to celebrate the anointing of a king.

We can begin to experience the significance of Mark's teaching about the baptism as anointing Jesus as king by exploring the coronation of kings and queens in history and in today's world.

AIMS

- to build on our images of kings and queens;
- to help us understand the images of coronation;
- to see the baptism of Jesus as proclamation of his kingship.

EXPLORING WITH CHILDREN

STARTING

Bring in pictures of the Queen's coronation or the Crown Jewels, or else bring in a paper crown. Discuss how a queen or king is crowned, drawing out ideas of:

- pictures of coronations the children have seen;
- special clothes worn;
- special items such as the crown, the rod, the sceptre;
- promises made by the king or queen;
- anointing with oil by the Archbishop.

TALKING POINTS

Tell the story from Mark of Jesus' baptism. As you work, talk with the children about the significance of the words from heaven. You could include the following points:

- a voice from heaven spoke at Jesus' baptism;
- the voice called him God's beloved son;
- kings of Israel were called God's son;
- this was an announcement that Jesus was king;
- Jesus' baptism was like a coronation.

ACTIVITIES

- Make cardboard crowns. Inside them you could write 'Jesus is King'.
- Make coronation robes to wear to the service. Use old curtains or sheets. Glue on decorations from felt.
- Shape aluminium foil or modelling material to make a copy of the container used for the anointing oil at the Queen's coronation.
- Act out Jesus' baptism. Use crêpe paper or Cellophane streamers as the water.

DISPLAY

- Today's theme is Jesus' baptism.
- At Jesus' baptism he was proclaimed king.
- Kings and queens are anointed at their coronations.
- Jesus is King.
- Our work today is about coronation.

EXPLORING WITH ADULTS

EXPERIENCE

- What are your experiences of coronation, in real life or on film?
- What public feelings are associated with coronations?
- How is the anointing given importance at coronations?

GOSPEL

- What does this gospel reading tell us about Mark's understanding of Jesus' baptism?
- How do you interpret this message for today?
- What does this account say about the person of Jesus?

APPLICATION

- How can your church affirm the kingship of Jesus?
- How can you affirm the kingship of Jesus?
- How can liturgy celebrate the kingship of Jesus?

CELEBRATING TOGETHER

WELCOMING CHILDREN

At an appropriate point in the service, invite the children to present their work on coronation. If they have made coronation robes, invite them to wear these robes as the story of Jesus' baptism is retold.

HYMNS AND SONGS

Come and Praise
  35 Praise the Lord! you heav'ns, adore him
  41 Fill thou my life

Hymns Ancient and Modern New Standard
142 Hail to the Lord's Anointed
348 Come, Lord, to our souls come down

21
DOVE

PREPARATION

GOSPEL THEME

Jesus' baptism (Luke 3.15–17, 21–22)

The gospel reading is Luke's account of the baptism of Jesus. More than the other evangelists, Luke emphasizes the role of the Holy Spirit in Jesus' baptism. In Luke's account, the Holy Spirit descended upon Jesus *in bodily form* like a dove. The words spoken by the voice from heaven, 'You are my Son', echo Psalm 2, a psalm used to celebrate the anointing of kings.

We can begin to experience the significance of Luke's teaching about the role of the Holy Spirit in Jesus' baptism by exploring the power of the image of the dove as a symbol for the Holy Spirit.

AIMS

● to build on our image of the dove;
● to see the dove as a symbol for the Holy Spirit;
● to understand the Holy Spirit as anointing Jesus at his baptism.

EXPLORING WITH CHILDREN

STARTING

Bring in a picture of a dove, perhaps on a Christmas card. Talk about doves, drawing out ideas of:

● anything the children know about doves;
● places the children have seen images of doves;
● jewellery or stickers they may own showing doves;
● the dove is used as a Christian symbol;
● the dove is a symbol of the Holy Spirit.

TALKING POINTS

Tell the story from Luke of Jesus' baptism. As you work, talk with the children about the significance of the dove. You could include the following points:

● Jesus was baptized with a crowd of people;
● his baptism was different;
● a dove settled on him;
● the Bible says the dove was the Holy Spirit in bodily form;
● a voice from heaven spoke.

ACTIVITIES

- Make dove-shaped badges to give to everyone in the congregation.
- Work together to paint a large picture of a dove.
- Prepare 'eye-witness interviews' with people who saw Jesus being baptized.
- Make a dove collage. Draw a large stylized dove and inside it glue dove pictures from Christmas cards, wrapping paper and brochures.

DISPLAY

- Today's theme is Jesus' baptism.
- The Holy Spirit anointed Jesus at his baptism.
- The dove is a symbol for the Holy Spirit.
- We celebrate the dove as a Christian symbol.
- Our work today is about the dove.

EXPLORING WITH ADULTS

EXPERIENCE

- What are your experiences and images of the dove?
- What feelings and attitudes are associated with the dove?
- Why should the dove symbolize the Holy Spirit?

GOSPEL

- What does this gospel tell us about Luke's understanding of the baptism of Jesus?
- How do you interpret this message for today?
- What does this account say about the person of Jesus?

APPLICATION

- How can your church proclaim the activity of the Holy Spirit?
- How can you proclaim the activity of the Holy Spirit?
- How can liturgy use the image of the dove?

CELEBRATING TOGETHER

WELCOMING CHILDREN

At an appropriate point in the service, invite the children to present their work on the dove. If they have produced a large picture of the dove, invite them to hold this by the font as the story of Jesus' baptism is retold.

HYMNS AND SONGS

Come and Praise
- 1 Morning has broken
- 45 The journey of life

Hymns Ancient and Modern New Standard
- 376 In Christ there is no east or west
- 526 When Jesus came to Jordan

22 NAMES

PREPARATION

GOSPEL THEME

Renaming Simon (John 1.29–42)

The gospel reading is from John's account of the beginning of Jesus' ministry and concerns the call of the first disciples. This account is very different from that presented by the other evangelists. John's account shows how the disciples of the Baptist recognized in Jesus God's Messiah and followed him. In appointing Simon as his own disciple, Jesus changes his name and accordingly changes his character. Simon is now called Peter and 'Peter' means 'the rock'.

We can begin to experience the significance of John's teaching about the new name given to Simon by exploring our own perceptions of the power of names and of nicknames.

AIMS

- to build on our ideas about names;
- to see how names (especially nicknames) can reveal character;
- to understand how Jesus changed the disciple's name and character.

EXPLORING WITH CHILDREN

STARTING

Bring in a dictionary of names. (Borrow one from your local library.) Look at it together, drawing out ideas of:

- the meanings of the children's names;
- the meaning of your own name;
- nicknames that the children are called;
- why such nicknames are chosen;
- if they like or dislike these nicknames.

TALKING POINTS

Tell the story from John of Jesus meeting Peter. As you work, talk with the children about the significance of Simon Peter's new name. You could include the following points:

- Simon Peter became one of Jesus' special three disciples;
- he was often first to realize the truth about Jesus;
- he was one of the first at the empty tomb after Jesus' resurrection;
- he was one of the leaders of the early church;
- in this way he was a 'rock'.

ACTIVITIES

- Make large name labels. Provide card for the children to cut to shape. Punch a hole in the top and add ribbon and a pin. Encourage the children to write their preferred names or nicknames and to draw pictures of favourite activities.

- Make a name board, including the names of everyone in the group and adding the meaning.

- If the children in the group know each other well, assign to each child the name of one other in the group (keeping these names private). Ask them to think up a nickname for the given person and to write something about the person that explains why the nickname was chosen. Read out these pieces and let children guess who has been written about.

- Prepare a wall display or a book about Peter the rock, adding information about some of the things he did.

DISPLAY

- Today's theme is renaming Simon.
- Jesus named Simon 'the rock'.
- My name is important to me.
- Nicknames can tell you what I am like.
- Our work today is about names.

EXPLORING WITH ADULTS

EXPERIENCE

- What do names tell you about people?
- What are your experiences of nicknames?
- Do people live up to the names they are given?

GOSPEL

- What does this gospel tell you about the call of Simon?
- How do you interpret this message for today?
- What does the new name say about Simon's character?

APPLICATION

- What significance should your church give to people's names?
- What significance should you give to people's names?
- How can names be used in liturgy?

CELEBRATING TOGETHER

WELCOMING CHILDREN

At an appropriate part of the service, invite the children to present their work on names. If they have produced large name labels for themselves, invite them to wear these labels and to cluster round the font. Remind them that these names were given at their baptism when they were called to follow Jesus.

HYMNS AND SONGS

Come and Praise
   13 Oh praise Him!
   44 He who would valiant be

Hymns Ancient and Modern New Standard
   343 Be thou my vision
   519 We are your people

23 LADDERS

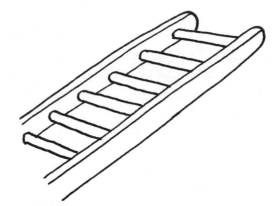

PREPARATION

GOSPEL THEME

Revelation (John 1.43–51)

The gospel reading is from John's account of the beginning of Jesus' ministry. On the previous day Andrew had followed Jesus and told his brother Simon. Today Philip follows Jesus and tells Nathanael. When Andrew followed Jesus he said 'We have found the Messiah'. When Nathanael followed Jesus he said 'You are the Son of God'. To both men the true identity of Jesus has been revealed. As Messiah and as Son of God Jesus becomes the way of communication between God and men and women. Jesus is like a ladder between heaven and earth along which the angels (God's messengers) travel.

We can begin to experience the significance of John's teaching about Jesus as the way of communication between God and men and women by exploring our own perceptions of ladders.

AIMS

● to build on our experiences of ladders;
● to see how ladders aid communication between different levels;
● to understand Jesus as the ladder between God and men and women.

EXPLORING WITH CHILDREN

STARTING

Bring in a stepladder. Let the children use it to reach high shelves. Discuss ladders, drawing out ideas of:

● times the children have used ladders;
● reasons for which we use ladders;
● places for which they are needed;
● what we use when ladders are not available;
● if substitutes are as safe and useful as ladders.

TALKING POINTS

Tell the story from John of Nathanael finding out Jesus' identity. As you work, talk with the children about the significance of who Jesus is. You could include the following points:

● the Jews had been promised a Messiah sent from God;
● they had been waiting for him for many years;
● Nathanael recognized Jesus as the Messiah, the Son of God;
● through Jesus we can talk to God;
● Jesus is like a ladder between heaven and earth.

ACTIVITIES

- Make a model of a ladder out of cardboard or scrap wood. On each rung write a different title for Jesus.
- Draw a ladder. Make up a prayer to write on the rungs, one word or one sentence to each rung.
- Cut a large ten-runged ladder out of cardboard. Write the name 'Jesus' twice down the rungs, one letter per rung. Walk along the rungs as the music plays and then down the other side. When the music stops, children standing on a letter must think of something to say about Jesus (a word or a sentence) beginning with that letter.
- Act out the story of Nathanael meeting Jesus.

DISPLAY

- Today's theme is revelation.
- Nathanael recognized Jesus as the Son of God.
- Jesus is like a ladder between heaven and earth.
- We need ladders to reach new heights.
- Our work today is about ladders.

EXPLORING WITH ADULTS

EXPERIENCE

- What are your experiences of ladders?
- How useful is the ladder as a symbol for communication?
- How helpful is the image of Jesus as the ladder?

GOSPEL

- What does this gospel tell us about John's understanding of Jesus?
- How do you interpret this message for today?
- How do you interpret John's reference to angels?

APPLICATION

- How should the church present Jesus as the ladder between heaven and earth today?
- How should you see Jesus as the ladder between heaven and earth today?
- How should this image of the ladder be used in liturgy?

CELEBRATING TOGETHER

WELCOMING CHILDREN

At an appropriate part in the service, invite the children to present their work on ladders. If they have sculptured a ladder, this should be set up in the church to symbolize communication between heaven and earth.

HYMNS AND SONGS

Come and Praise
  87 Give us hope, Lord
  96 A still small voice in the heart of the city

Hymns Ancient and Modern New Standard
249 Take my life, and let it be
485 Lord, as I wake I turn to you

24
WEDDING RECEPTION

PREPARATION

GOSPEL THEME

Wedding at Cana (John 2.1–11)

John's account of the wedding at Cana comes immediately after the first disciples follow Jesus. When wine runs out, Jesus replenishes the supply. In verse 11 John explains why he starts with this story: it 'is the first of the signs by which Jesus revealed his glory and led his disciples to believe in him'. It is no accident that the first *sign* takes place at a wedding feast. In Jewish thought the wedding feast is a way of speaking about God's kingdom, when the Messiah will preside at the banquet.

We can begin to experience the significance of John's teaching about Jesus at the wedding at Cana by exploring our own perceptions of wedding receptions.

AIMS

● to build on our experiences and ideas of wedding receptions;

● to understand the biblical image of the wedding feast;

● to see the wedding at Cana as celebrating Jesus as Messiah.

EXPLORING WITH CHILDREN

STARTING

Bring in wedding photographs or pictures. Discuss wedding receptions, drawing out ideas of:

● weddings the children have attended;

● wedding receptions they have stayed to;

● what happens at a wedding reception;

● the food and drink at the reception;

● a wedding reception as a time to celebrate.

TALKING POINTS

Tell the story from John of the wedding at Cana. As you work, talk with the children about the significance of this wedding. You could include the following points:

● Jesus turned the water into wine;

● this helped the disciples know him as the Messiah, the Son of God;

● the wedding feast was an important picture to Jews;

● they thought of God's kingdom as being like a wedding feast with the Messiah in charge;

● Jesus showed his power at this wedding.

ACTIVITIES

- Prepare some special food to share with each other or with the congregation as a celebration feast.
- Make a mural of either a wedding reception or the wedding at Cana.
- Dress up as a bride and groom and as guests at a wedding.
- Bring in a large sponge cake or enough small cakes for the children. Ice the cake or cakes, decorating them to look like a wedding cake.

DISPLAY

- Today's theme is the wedding at Cana.
- Jesus showed his power at the wedding.
- Jesus' disciples knew he was the Messiah.
- We celebrate at church just like at a wedding feast.
- Our work today is about wedding receptions.

EXPLORING WITH ADULTS

EXPERIENCE

- What are your experiences of wedding receptions?
- What feelings and moods are conveyed by wedding receptions?
- How does the wedding reception become a symbol for the Kingdom of God?

GOSPEL

- What does this gospel tell us about signs of God's glory?
- How do you interpret this message for today?

- How do you understand the wedding at Cana?

APPLICATION

- How should the church present the wedding at Cana today?
- How should you use this sign today?
- How should the sign of the wedding at Cana be used in liturgy?

CELEBRATING TOGETHER

WELCOMING CHILDREN

At an appropriate point in the service, invite the children to present their work on wedding receptions. If they have produced a mural about the wedding reception, this can be used as an altar frontal to emphasis the link between the wedding at Cana and the eucharist.

HYMNS AND SONGS

Come and Praise
- 14 All the nations of the earth
- 32 Thank you, Lord, for this new day

Hymns Ancient and Modern New Standard
- 95 Holy, holy, holy! Lord God Almighty!
- 439 Christ is the heavenly food that gives

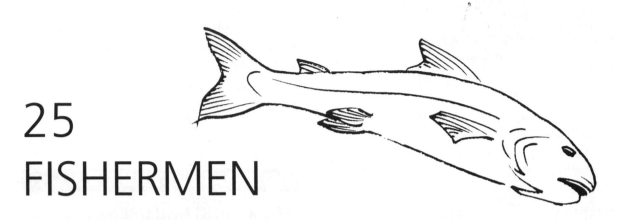

25
FISHERMEN

PREPARATION

GOSPEL THEME

First disciples (Matthew 4.12–23)

The gospel reading is Matthew's account of the call of the first four disciples, Simon and Andrew, James and John. According to the tradition, these four men had worked as fishermen. Jesus called them away from their established trade and called them 'to fish for people'. Fishing for people is a powerful image for the task of the early disciples during the ministry of Jesus. It remains a powerful image for disciples in today's world as well.

We can begin to experience the significance of Jesus calling his disciples to fish for people by exploring our own ideas about the work of fishermen.

AIMS

- to build on our ideas about fishermen;
- to understand Jesus' call to fish for people;
- to share in the work of Jesus' disciples.

EXPLORING WITH CHILDREN

STARTING

Bring in a fishing rod and tackle, or pictures of these. Discuss fishing, drawing out ideas of:

- any fishing experiences the children have had;
- any fishing experiences you have had;
- fishing stories they have heard;
- why we need fishermen;
- some of Jesus' disciples were fishermen.

TALKING POINTS

Tell the story from Matthew of Jesus choosing his disciples. As you work, talk with the children about the significance of this choosing. You could include the following points:

- Simon, Andrew, James and John were fishermen;
- Jesus chose them to be his disciples;
- he told them they would 'fish for people';
- they followed him immediately;
- we can still 'fish for people' today.

ACTIVITIES

- Make a sea display. Each child could cut out and decorate a fish to add to the display. Add twisted strips of blue Cellophane to give the impression of water.
- Make a fishing game. Write out twenty names from the Bible, including the names of the disciples. Add a paperclip to each name and put them in a box. The children fish for the names with a magnet attached to a pole by a piece of twine. As they read each name they must say if it is a disciple or someone else.
- Make special invitations to give to friends, inviting them to come to church with you one week.
- Make 'Wanted' posters, asking for modern 'fishers of men'.

DISPLAY

- Today's theme is the first disciples.
- Simon, Andrew, James and John were fishermen.
- The disciples were called to be 'fishers of men'.
- We can share in the work of Jesus' disciples.
- Our work today is about fishermen.

EXPLORING WITH ADULTS

EXPERIENCE

- What are your experiences of fishing?
- What are your ideas and images about fishermen?
- How do fishermen become a symbol for the work of a disciple?

GOSPEL

- What does the gospel tell us about the first disciples?
- How do you interpret this message for today?
- How do you understand the call to fish for people?

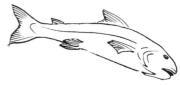

APPLICATION

- How should the church present the call to fish for people today?
- How should you respond to the call to fish for people?
- How should the call to fish for people be used in liturgy?

CELEBRATING TOGETHER

WELCOMING CHILDREN

At an appropriate point in the service, invite the children to present their work on fishermen. Have prepared some fishing nets and display these while an appropriate hymn is sung.

HYMNS AND SONGS

Come and Praise
  22 I danced in the morning
  34 Praise to the Lord

Hymns Ancient and Modern New Standard
  312 Jesus calls us: o'er the tumult
  392 Lord Jesus, once you spoke to men

26 MAKING WINE

PREPARATION

GOSPEL THEME

Wedding at Cana (John 2.1–11)

John's account of the wedding at Cana comes immediately after the first disciples follow Jesus. When the wine runs out, Jesus replenishes the supply. In verse 11 John explains why he starts with this story: it 'is the first of the signs by which Jesus revealed his glory and led his disciples to believe in him'. It is no accident that the first *sign* takes place at a wedding feast. In Jewish thought the wedding feast is a way of speaking about God's Kingdom, when the Messiah will preside at the banquet.

We can begin to experience the significance of John's teaching about the wine at the wedding at Cana by exploring our own perceptions of wine making.

AIMS

- to build on our experiences and ideas of making wine;
- to understand the biblical image of wine at the wedding feast;
- to see the wine at the wedding feast as celebrating Jesus as Messiah.

EXPLORING WITH CHILDREN

STARTING

Bring in some wine-making equipment or a bunch of grapes. Talk about making wine, drawing out ideas of:

- home-made wine can be made from most fruits;
- the wine we buy is generally made from grapes;
- experiences you or the children have had of making wine;
- wine is made from fermented fruit;
- the early process is fun to watch even if they cannot drink it.

TALKING POINTS

Tell the story from John of Jesus turning water into wine. As you work, talk with the children about the significance of Jesus' action. You could include the following points:

- Jesus was at a wedding when the wine ran out;
- he told the servants to fill large jars with water;
- this water became wine;
- God's kingdom was spoken of as a wedding feast;
- because of this sign the disciples believed in Jesus.

ACTIVITIES

- Begin a wine fermentation jar so that the children can see the process.
- Alternatively, allow the children to see the same process with yeast, flour and water in small jars to take home.
- Act out the story of the wedding at Cana.
- Make invitations to the 'wedding feast' of God's Kingdom, where we will celebrate Jesus as Messiah.

DISPLAY

- Today's theme is the wedding at Cana.
- Jesus' first sign of his glory was at a wedding.
- Jesus turned water into wine.
- Wine is a symbol of celebration.
- Our work today is about making wine.

EXPLORING WITH ADULTS

EXPERIENCE

- What are your experiences of making wine?
- What is special about having wine at feasts?
- How does wine at the wedding become a symbol for the Kingdom of God?

GOSPEL

- What does this gospel tell us about signs of God's glory?
- How do you interpret this message for today?
- How do you understand the transformation of water into wine?

APPLICATION

- How should the church present the transformation of water into wine today?
- How should you apply this sign today?
- How should the sign of water into wine be used in liturgy?

CELEBRATING TOGETHER

WELCOMING CHILDREN

At an appropriate point in the service, invite the children to present their work on wine making. If they have started a fermentation jar, this can be carried in the offertory procession alongside the wine brought for the eucharist.

HYMNS AND SONGS

Come and Praise
   3 All things bright and beautiful
 90 I come like a beggar

Hymns Ancient and Modern New Standard
115 Dear Lord and Father of mankind
224 Lead us, heavenly Father, lead us

27 SCROLLS

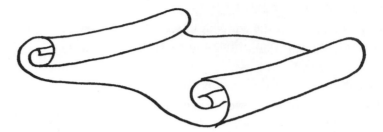

GOSPEL THEME

Synagogue at Nazareth (Luke 4.14–21)

Luke begins his account of Jesus' ministry not with the call of the first disciples, but with Jesus returning to his home town of Nazareth and teaching in the synagogue there. In this passage Luke is concerned to show that Jesus' ministry was clearly foretold in the Old Testament. The very same Holy Spirit who inspired God's people in the Old Testament is now anointing Jesus to do the work of God. The message of continuity with the past is symbolized by the scroll of the prophet Isaiah.

We can begin to experience the significance of Luke's concern to demonstrate that Jesus is continuing and extending the work which God began in the Old Testament by exploring our images of history associated with the ancient scrolls.

AIMS

● to build on our ideas about ancient scrolls;

● to develop our sense of Jesus' location in history;

● to see Jesus continuing and extending God's work in the Old Testament.

STARTING

Bring in a scroll or a picture of a scroll. Discuss this, drawing out ideas of:

● scrolls or pictures the children have seen;

● times the children have made scrolls;

● the use of scrolls in ancient times before books;

● the books in our Bible were first written on scrolls;

● today we use the word 'scroll' for pastries like coffee scrolls and for looking through documents on a computer.

TALKING POINTS

Tell the story from Luke of Jesus in the synagogue. As you work, talk with the children about the significance of Jesus' work. You could include the following points:

● the Old Testament tells us about God's work;

● God's work involved justice and help for those in need;

● in the Old Testament, God promised to send a Messiah;

● Jesus was that promised one;

● Jesus continued God's work that was begun in Old Testament times.

ACTIVITIES

- Work together to make and decorate a large scroll. While some children prepare and decorate the wooden rolls, others could write on paper the words of Luke 4.18–19.

- Prepare a time line to show Jesus' place in history. Ask the children to draw pictures of the different Bible characters they know. Display these named pictures along a wall in their chronological order.

- Bake fruit scrolls. Bring in a batch of sweet dough, roll it up with fruit and spices inside, slice and bake it.

- Prepare a display of information about Christians today who continue God's work as expressed in Luke 4.

DISPLAY

- Today's theme is the synagogue at Nazareth.
- Jesus read from a scroll.
- Jesus continued God's work.
- We can continue God's work today.
- Our work today is about scrolls.

EXPLORING WITH ADULTS

EXPERIENCE

- What is your experience of ancient scrolls?
- What do scrolls suggest to you?
- How are scrolls used in the synagogue today?

GOSPEL

- What does this gospel tell us about Luke's understanding of Jesus?
- How do you interpret this message for today?

- What were the activities of the anointed one foretold by Isaiah?

APPLICATION

- How should the church proclaim the work of God's anointed one today?
- How should you acknowledge the work of God's anointed one today?
- How should the work of God's anointed one be celebrated in liturgy?

CELEBRATING TOGETHER

WELCOMING CHILDREN

At an appropriate point in the service, invite the children to present their work on scrolls. If they have made a scroll for use in liturgy, use this scroll to proclaim some verses from Scripture.

HYMNS AND SONGS

Come and Praise
  13 Oh praise Him!
147 Make me a channel of your peace

Hymns Ancient and Modern New Standard
233 O thou who camest from above
382 Jesus our Lord, our King and our God

28 FAVOURITE DRINKS

PREPARATION

GOSPEL THEME

Wedding at Cana (John 2.1–11)

John's account of the wedding at Cana comes immediately after the first disciples follow Jesus. When the wine runs out, Jesus replenishes the supply. In verse 11 John explains why he starts with this story: it 'is the first of the signs by which Jesus revealed his glory and led his disciples to believe in him'. It is no accident that the first *sign* takes place at a wedding feast. In Jewish thought the wedding feast is a way of speaking about God's Kingdom, when the Messiah will preside at the banquet

We can begin to experience the significance of John's teaching about the wine at the wedding at Cana by exploring our own perceptions of our favourite drinks.

AIMS

- to build on our experiences of favourite drinks;
- to understand the significance of wine at the wedding feast;
- to see the wine as celebrating Jesus' Messiahship at the wedding feast.

EXPLORING WITH CHILDREN

STARTING

Bring in a selection of different drinks. Discuss these, drawing out ideas of:

- those the children have tasted;
- other drinks the children have tried;
- drinks the children would like to try;
- the children's favourite drinks;
- different drinks for when we are hot, cold or at a party.

TALKING POINTS

Tell the story from John of the wedding at Cana. As you work, talk with the children about the significance of this wedding. You could include the following points:

- Jesus turned the water into wine;
- this helped the disciples know him as the Messiah, the Son of God;
- the wedding feast was an important picture to Jewish people;
- it was a picture of God's Kingdom;
- Jesus showed his power at this wedding.

ACTIVITIES

- Make your own fruit drink. Mix together the juice of two lemons and two oranges, four tablespoons of sugar and four cups of water.
- Make a selection of drinks, hot and cold, to serve after the service. Ask people about their favourite drinks and fill in a graph of the results.
- Prepare adverts for your own favourite drinks.
- Plan interviews with the disciples about the events of the wedding and their reactions.

DISPLAY

- Today's theme is the wedding at Cana.
- Jesus turned water into wine.
- Wine is a symbol of celebration.
- Jesus showed his power at the wedding.
- Our work today is about favourite drinks.

EXPLORING WITH ADULTS

EXPERIENCE

- What are your favourite drinks?
- How are certain drinks associated with special events or feelings?
- What special significance does wine have at the wedding feast?

GOSPEL

- What does the gospel tell us about wine at the wedding?
- How do you interpret this message for today?
- What is special about the new wine?

APPLICATION

- What should the church teach about wine today?
- How should this story affect your life today?
- How should the images of water and wine be used in liturgy?

CELEBRATING TOGETHER

WELCOMING CHILDREN

At an appropriate point in the service, invite the children to present their work on favourite drinks. If the children have assembled a range of different drinks, the congregation can be invited to stay for a 'drink tasting' session after the service. Small plastic cups are ideal for this.

HYMNS AND SONGS

Come and Praise
  20 Come, my brothers, praise the Lord
  59 I will bring to you

Hymns Ancient and Modern New Standard
258 Author of life divine
271 Bread of heaven, on thee we feed

29
JIGSAW PUZZLE

PREPARATION

GOSPEL THEME

Exorcism at Capernaum (Mark 1.21–28)

In Mark's gospel, after Jesus has called the first four disciples he moves directly on to performing four major acts of healing. The exorcism in the synagogue is the first of these healings. On this occasion an unclean spirit is driven out of the man. At the same time the unclean spirit recognizes Jesus as the Holy One of God. Throughout these healings Mark is concerned to show how Jesus brings both health and wholeness to those whose lives are fragmented.

We can begin to experience the significance of Mark's message about health and wholeness by exploring how jigsaw puzzles can be either fragmented or integrated.

AIMS

- to build on our experiences of jigsaw puzzles;
- to help us understand the wholeness when the puzzle is completed;
- to see the healing which Jesus offers as a form of wholeness.

EXPLORING WITH CHILDREN

STARTING

Bring in a simple jigsaw puzzle and ask the children to help you assemble it. Discuss jigsaw puzzles, drawing out ideas of:

- other jigsaw puzzles the children have worked on;
- the hardest jigsaw puzzle they have completed;
- any feelings of frustration they experience while they work;
- the feeling of satisfaction when the puzzle is completed;
- a jigsaw puzzle is whole or complete when it is assembled.

TALKING POINTS

Tell the story from Mark of the exorcism. As you work, talk with the children about the significance of health and wholeness. You could include the following points:

- Jesus healed many people in many ways;
- some people were ill or had physical problems;
- this man had an unclean spirit within him;
- Jesus cast out the unclean spirit and gave the man health;
- Jesus restored people to wholeness in body and mind.

ACTIVITIES

- Make your own jigsaw puzzle. Glue a picture onto cardboard. Draw a cutting pattern on the back of the cardboard and then cut along these lines.

- Play a guessing game. Show each other a few pieces from simple jigsaw puzzles and see if the others can guess what the whole picture is. Assemble these puzzles to see if any guesses were correct.

- Draw the Bible story in cartoon form.

- Plan a dance about the wholeness that Jesus offers. Individuals could dance separately, getting in each other's way and causing chaos. Gradually one person could join with another until all are joined and dancing together.

DISPLAY

- Today's theme is the exorcism at Capernaum.
- Jesus offered healing and wholeness.
- Jesus healed a man with an unclean spirit.
- When a jigsaw puzzle is completed, we see the whole.
- Our work today is about jigsaw puzzles.

EXPLORING WITH ADULTS

EXPERIENCE

- What are your experiences of jigsaw puzzles?
- How do you feel when the last piece of the jigsaw has been put in place?
- How useful is the jigsaw puzzle as an image of wholeness?

GOSPEL

- What does this gospel say about Jesus' power over unclean spirits?
- How do you interpret this message for today?
- What do you understand by unclean spirits?

APPLICATION

- How should the church respond to unclean spirits today?
- How should you respond to unclean spirits today?
- How should the church's ministry of healing be related to liturgy?

CELEBRATING TOGETHER

WELCOMING CHILDREN

At an appropriate point in the service, invite the children to present their work on jigsaw puzzles. Have the pieces of a large jigsaw puzzle scattered on a prominent table. Invite the congregation to stay after the service to solve this jigsaw puzzle.

HYMNS AND SONGS

Come and Praise
  30 Join with us
  52 Lord of all hopefulness

Hymns Ancient and Modern New Standard
  95 Holy, holy, holy! Lord God Almighty!
  444 Christians, lift up your hearts

30 LIGHTS

PREPARATION

GOSPEL THEME

Presentation in the temple (Luke 2.22–40)

Luke's account of Jesus' infancy takes Mary, Joseph and the infant Jesus to the temple in Jerusalem for the ceremony of the purification of the mother forty days after the birth. In the temple the Holy Spirit inspires Simeon and Anna to prophesy about the infant Jesus' future. In verse 32 Simeon speaks of Jesus as a light bringing God's salvation to the Gentiles as well as to the Jewish people.

We can begin to experience the significance of Simeon's image of Jesus as a light by exploring our own experiences of light.

AIMS

- to build on our experiences and ideas of light;
- to understand the biblical image of Jesus as a light;
- to see Jesus as a light revealing God's purposes to the Gentiles.

EXPLORING WITH CHILDREN

STARTING

Bring in a torch and a candle. Discuss these and other lights, drawing out ideas of:

- lights the children use in the home;
- lights the children use outside;
- any other sources of light that can be used;
- the comfort that light gives us;
- the way light shines out in the darkness.

TALKING POINTS

Tell the story from Luke of Jesus' presentation in the temple. As you work, talk with the children about the significance of Jesus as a light. You could include the following points:

- Simeon described Jesus as a light to all people;
- Simeon and Jesus lived in a world with few lights;
- light shines out clearly in the darkness;
- light reveals what is around it;
- Jesus reveals God's purpose and glory.

ACTIVITIES

- Make your own candles. Your local library should be able to tell you several different methods. Choose one that is safe for children. You may need extra adult helpers.
- Make a large poster showing pictures of different lights. These can be painted by the children or cut from magazines.
- Write words such as 'Jesus is the light of the world' using wax crayons in yellows and reds. Paint over the paper with diluted black paint so that the 'light' shines through.
- Make a display of different lights or make clay or papier mâché models.

DISPLAY

- Today's theme is the Presentation in the temple.
- Simeon called Jesus a light to all people.
- Jesus reveals God's purposes.
- Light shines in the darkness.
- Our work today is about lights.

EXPLORING WITH ADULTS

EXPERIENCE

- What are your experiences of light?
- What is the significance of light as a symbol?
- How do you think of Jesus as a light?

GOSPEL

- What does the gospel tell us about Jesus as a light?
- How do you interpret this message for today?
- How do you understand Jesus as a light to the Gentiles?

APPLICATION

- How should the church present the image of Jesus as light today?
- How should the image of Jesus as light shape your own spirituality?
- How can Simeon's song best be used in liturgy today?

CELEBRATING TOGETHER

WELCOMING CHILDREN

At an appropriate point in the service, invite the children to present their work on light. If the children have made candles appropriate for use in procession, a procession can be arranged after the gospel reading and while Simeon's song is being sung.

HYMNS AND SONGS

Come and Praise
- 8 Let us with a gladsome mind
- 29 From the darkness came light

Hymns Ancient and Modern New Standard
- 342 Awake, awake: fling off the night!
- 440 Christ is the world's light, he and none other

31 SALT

PREPARATION

GOSPEL THEME

Salt of the earth (Matthew 5.13–20)

After the beatitudes, Matthew's Sermon on the Mount continues with two important images employed to describe those who accept the way of the new law. They are the salt of the earth. They are the light of the world. Jesus' teaching in the Sermon on the Mount challenges his hearers to live up to the new way of life which they have accepted.

We can begin to experience the significance of Matthew's image about the salt of the earth by exploring our own understanding of the properties of salt.

AIMS

- to build on our experiences of salt;
- to help us understand the effect salt has on other things;
- to respond to Jesus' invitation to be salt of the earth.

EXPLORING WITH CHILDREN

STARTING

Pass around a salt shaker or some salted potato crisps and invite the children to taste. Discuss what the children know about salt, drawing out ideas of:

- food that is improved by salt;
- food that they definitely would not put salt on;
- the use of salt to preserve food;
- the importance of salt in countries without refrigeration;
- our need for extra salt when we perspire a lot.

TALKING POINTS

Tell the children Jesus' words about salt from Matthew. As you work, talk with the children about the significance of Christians as salt of the earth. You could include the following points:

- salt makes a difference to food;
- Christians make a difference to the world;
- salt dissolves easily in liquid and changes it;
- Christians need to be part of the world, changing it;
- Jesus invites us to be the salt of the earth.

ACTIVITIES

- Make a food collage with pictures from magazines or supermarket adverts. On one side glue foods that need salt and on the other glue those without salt.
- Make salt dough sculptures. The salt preserves the articles. Mix together two cups of plain flour, one cup of salt and one cup of water. Shape your sculptures and bake in the oven at 190°C (375°F) for about an hour until dry.
- Write poems about salt. They could be about salt in food or about Christians as salt of the earth.
- Conduct some experiments. Use a small amount of water and see how much salt you can dissolve in it. Add a small amount of salt to a large amount of liquid and see how quickly it changes the taste.

DISPLAY

- Today's theme is the salt of the earth.
- We need salt in our lives.
- The world needs Christians.
- We are called to be like salt in the world.
- Our work today is about salt.

EXPLORING WITH ADULTS

EXPERIENCE

- What are your experiences of salt?
- How does salt affect other things?
- Why is salt so precious?

GOSPEL

- What does this gospel say about the followers of Jesus?

- How do you interpret this message for today?
- What is the significance of salt for God's people?

APPLICATION

- How should the church respond to the image of salt today?
- How should you respond to the image of salt today?
- How can the image of salt be used in liturgy?

CELEBRATING TOGETHER

WELCOMING CHILDREN

At an appropriate point in the service, invite the children to present their work on salt. If they have composed poems on salt, invite them to read these poems. Develop a short responsorial prayer about the people of God as salt.

HYMNS AND SONGS

Come and Praise
49 We are climbing Jesus' ladder, ladder
103 I am planting my feet in the footsteps

Hymns Ancient and Modern New Standard
149 Ye servants of God, your master proclaim
346 Christ is the world's true light

32
HEALTH CENTRE

GOSPEL THEME

Simon's mother-in-law (Mark 1.29–39)

In Mark's gospel, after Jesus has called the first four disciples he moves directly on to performing four major acts of healing. The restoration of Simon's mother-in-law is the second of these healings. This time a sick woman is cured of a fever. The cure is so effective that she gets up and waits on her visitors. Mark is concerned to show that Jesus is victorious over the fevers which destroy human life.

We can begin to deepen our understanding of Mark's message about Jesus the healer by exploring our own perceptions of the local health centre.

AIMS

● to build on our experiences of local health centres;
● to see how health centres offer a range of healings;
● to recognize Jesus the healer.

STARTING

Bring in a poster or booklet from your local health centre. Discuss the children's own experiences of the health centre, drawing out ideas of:

● people who work at the health centre;
● different tasks of the centre, such as baby clinics;
● illnesses the children have had;
● who helped them;
● some people have no health centres to visit.

TALKING POINTS

Tell the story from Mark of Jesus healing Simon's mother-in-law. As you work, talk with the children about the significance of Jesus' work. You could include the following points:

● in Jesus' time there were very few doctors;
● most people could not afford to see a doctor;
● there were many people with illnesses;
● Jesus healed many who were ill;
● people came a long way to see him and be healed.

ACTIVITIES

- Make a mural of the work of the health centre.
- Make clothes and equipment to dress up as doctors and nurses.
- Write an article for the 'Galilee Gazette' about Jesus' healing work. You could include an interview with a doctor of the time.
- Make a book about your own local health centre, with a page for each person the children know. Write about the person and about his or her work.

DISPLAY

- Today's theme is Simon's mother-in-law.
- Jesus healed many people.
- Our health centre helps people who are ill.
- Jesus is the great healer.
- Our work today is about the health centre.

EXPLORING WITH ADULTS

EXPERIENCE

- What are your experiences of local health centres?
- What is the range of therapies available through the health centre?
- How does Jesus offer healing?

GOSPEL

- What does this gospel say about Jesus' power over fevers?
- How do you interpret this message for today?
- What do you understand by Simon's mother-in-law's fever?

APPLICATION

- How should the church respond to fevers today?
- How should you respond to fevers today?
- How should the church pray for healing in liturgy?

CELEBRATING TOGETHER

WELCOMING CHILDREN

At an appropriate point in the service, invite the children to present their work on the health centre. If they have made a mural of the health centre, this can be displayed while the story of the healing of Simon's mother-in-law is retold.

HYMNS AND SONGS

Come and Praise
  24 Go, tell it on the mountain
101 In the bustle of the city

Hymns Ancient and Modern New Standard
    9 At even, ere the sun was set
286 From thee all skill and science flow

33 FISH

GOSPEL THEME

The great catch (Luke 5.1–11)

In Luke's gospel, after Jesus left Nazareth he cured the possessed man at Capernaum and healed Simon's mother-in-law before attracting his team of close followers. This gospel reading is Luke's account of how Simon, James and John came to leave their trade as fishermen to be followers of Jesus. Just as they were to catch many people for the Kingdom, so Jesus enabled them to land a large catch of fish.

We can begin to experience the significance of Luke's teaching about the large catch of fish by exploring our own perceptions of fish in all their variety.

AIMS

- to build on our experiences of fish;
- to help us understand the significance of the great catch of fish;
- to share in the disciples' commission to catch people.

STARTING

Bring in a fresh fish (from the supermarket) or some fishing tackle or a can of tuna. Talk with the children about their experiences with fish, drawing out ideas of:

- any fishing they have done;
- how fish are caught;
- fish they enjoy eating;
- the food value in fish;
- some of Jesus' disciples were fishermen.

TALKING POINTS

Tell the story from Luke of the great catch of fish. As you work, talk with the children about the significance of this. You could include the following points:

- the fishermen had already caught nothing;
- they trusted Jesus and tried again;
- they caught more fish than they could handle;
- they followed Jesus and learned how to 'fish' for people;
- we too can 'fish' for people.

ACTIVITIES

- Cut out and decorate fish in all shapes and sizes. Refer to fishing books from the library for shapes and colours.
- Make a model of the lake with the boats, fish and fishermen.
- Make an invitation in the shape of a fish. Inside write details about your church and use it to invite a friend to come with you.
- Devise a fishing dance, with some children as fishermen and women and some as fish.

DISPLAY

- Today's theme is the great catch.
- The disciples learned about catching people.
- We, too, can 'fish' for people.
- Jesus chose fishermen to work with him.
- Our work today is about fish.

EXPLORING WITH ADULTS

EXPERIENCE

- What are your experiences of fish?
- How many different kinds of fish do you know?
- What do you know about fish in Palestine?

GOSPEL

- What does this gospel tell us about the first disciples?
- How do you interpret this message for today?
- What is the significance of the great catch?

APPLICATION

- How should the church celebrate those first disciples today?
- How can you celebrate those first disciples today?
- What place is there for the great catch of fish in liturgy?

CELEBRATING TOGETHER

WELCOMING CHILDREN

At an appropriate point in the service, invite the children to present their work on fish. If they have made many cut-out shapes of fish, invite them to place these fish in a large net while the story of the great catch is being retold.

HYMNS AND SONGS

Come and Praise
105 God of the morning
136 We thank you Lord for all we eat

Hymns Ancient and Modern New Standard
181 May the grace of Christ our Saviour
444 Christians, lift up your hearts

34 ANGER

PREPARATION

GOSPEL THEME

The better way (Matthew 5.21–37)

In the Sermon on the Mount, Jesus compares and contrasts the teaching of the old law with the teaching of the new law. While the old law was concerned with the outward acts, the new law is concerned with the inward thoughts. While the old law spoke out against murder, the new law speaks out against anger. Jesus' teaching in the Sermon on the Mount challenges his hearers to live up to the new way of life which they have accepted.

We can begin to experience the significance of Matthew's teaching about the new law by exploring our own understanding of anger.

AIMS

● to build on our experiences of anger;
● to see how anger gives rise to evil actions;
● to respond to Jesus' invitation to follow the new law.

EXPLORING WITH CHILDREN

STARTING

Bring in a picture or a newspaper article about anger, or show an angry expression and ask the children to guess your feeling. Talk about anger, drawing out ideas of:

● times the children have been angry;
● things that make them angry;
● things that make their family or friends angry;
● the ways in which anger can hurt other people;
● times they have been hurt by the anger of others.

TALKING POINTS

Tell the children Jesus' words on anger from Matthew. As you work, talk with the children about the significance of his teaching. You could include the following points:

● we often talk about wrong actions;
● Jesus said wrong thoughts are just as bad;
● being angry can be just as bad as killing;
● anger can be like killing with our thoughts;
● we need to make peace with people.

ACTIVITIES

- Make paper plate masks showing an angry face.
- Prepare a dance or drama on anger. Use loud music and strong movements. You could contrast this with a dance where a peacemaker steps in and gently touches people and calms them.
- Ask the children to paint anger. Encourage them to paint feelings and rhythms rather than people and real-life situations. Ask them about colours and movements associated with anger. If you prefer a contrast, some could paint peaceful pictures.
- Make decorated wall plaques of some of Jesus' words as a reminder to make peace.

DISPLAY

- Today's theme is the better way.
- Jesus said that anger can be like murder.
- It is better to make peace than to stay angry.
- Anger causes trouble.
- Our work today is about anger.

EXPLORING WITH ADULTS

EXPERIENCE

- What are your experiences of anger?
- How does anger give rise to actions?
- Why is anger so dangerous?

GOSPEL

- What does this gospel say about Jesus' goals for God's people?
- How do you interpret this message for today?

- What is the significance of leaving your gift before the altar?

APPLICATION

- How should the church respond to anger today?
- How should you respond to anger?
- How should anger be acknowledged in the liturgy?

CELEBRATING TOGETHER

WELCOMING CHILDREN

At an appropriate point in the service, invite the children to present their work on anger. If they have prepared a dance or drama on anger, this can be presented and summed up against the beatitude 'Blessed are the peacemakers'.

HYMNS AND SONGS

Come and Praise
  23 Jesus, good above all other
 102 You can't stop rain from falling down

Hymns Ancient and Modern New Standard
 312 'Forgive our sins as we forgive'
 367 God of grace and God of glory

35 HOSPITAL

PREPARATION

GOSPEL THEME

The healed leper (Mark 1.40–45)

In Mark's gospel, after Jesus has called the first four disciples, he moves directly on to performing four major acts of healing. The healing of the leper is the third of these healings. On this occasion Jesus touches the man and says 'Be made clean!' At the same time Jesus commands the man not to publicize the healing. Mark is concerned to show that Jesus is not intimidated by contagious or communicable disease.

We can further deepen our understanding of Mark's message about Jesus the healer by exploring our own perceptions of local hospitals.

AIMS

● to build on our experiences of local hospitals;

● to see the variety of ways in which patients are treated;

● to recognize Jesus' close contact with disease.

EXPLORING WITH CHILDREN

STARTING

Bring in a brochure from a local hospital or a picture of a hospital. Talk together about hospitals, drawing out ideas of:

● times the children have been patients in hospital;

● times the children have visited a hospital;

● the name and location of your local hospital;

● the various jobs of people in hospitals;

● some of the conditions that are treated in hospital.

TALKING POINTS

Tell the children the story from Mark of the healed leper. As you work, talk with the children about the significance of Jesus' work. You could include the following points:

● lepers were considered unclean and no one would touch them;

● they lived away from others;

● this leper believed Jesus could heal him;

● Jesus touched him;

● the leper became well.

ACTIVITIES

- Paint or decorate cards and balloons to be taken to the children's ward of the hospital as a gift. (Check first that this would be acceptable.)
- Write out the name, phone number and address of the local hospital on a card which will fit under the phone and can be used in emergencies.
- Make a list of the different units and wards in a hospital.
- Act out the story of the leper, with the villagers shooing him away and Jesus welcoming him.

DISPLAY

- Today's theme is the healed leper.
- Jesus touched and healed a leper.
- Jesus helped those who were ill.
- Our local hospital is a place of healing.
- Our work today is about the hospital.

EXPLORING WITH ADULTS

EXPERIENCE

- What are your experiences of local hospitals?
- What is the range of ways in which patients are treated?
- How does Jesus draw alongside the sick?

GOSPEL

- What does this gospel say about Jesus' power over leprosy?
- How do you interpret this message for today?
- What do you understand by the way Jesus touched the leper?

APPLICATION

- How should the church respond to communicable diseases today?
- How should you respond to those with communicable diseases?
- How should the church's response to communicable diseases be expressed in liturgy?

CELEBRATING TOGETHER

WELCOMING CHILDREN

At an appropriate point in the service, invite the children to present their work on the hospital. If they have made a list of the different units and wards in the hospital, this can be displayed while the story of the healing of the leper is retold.

HYMNS AND SONGS

Come and Praise
22 I danced in the morning
30 Join with us

Hymns Ancient and Modern New Standard
115 Dear Lord and Father
406 O God, by whose almighty plan

36
PROVERBS

PREPARATION

GOSPEL THEME

The Beatitudes (Luke 6.17–26)

Luke presents a collection of Jesus' teaching in a discourse delivered not on the mountain (as in Matthew), but on a level place. Like Matthew's Sermon on the Mount, Luke's Sermon on the Plain begins with a set of beatitudes, statements beginning 'Blessed are you'. In Luke's sermon these beatitudes are accompanied by a set of woes. The beatitudes and woes are well-shaped, easy to remember, sentences like proverbs.

We can begin to experience the significance of Jesus' method of teaching through beatitudes by exploring our understanding of proverbs and other well-known phrases and sayings.

AIMS

● to build on our experiences of proverbs and other phrases and sayings;
● to help us understand Jesus' method of teaching through beatitudes;
● to value the beatitudes of Jesus.

EXPLORING WITH CHILDREN

STARTING

Write out a few well-known proverbs such as 'A stitch in time saves nine'. Show these to the children and discuss them, drawing out ideas of:

● times the children have heard or read them;
● what they mean;
● the name for such sayings is 'proverbs';
● other proverbs the children have heard;
● whether or not such sayings are helpful.

TALKING POINTS

Tell the children the beatitudes from Luke. As you work, talk with the children about the significance of these beatitudes. You could include the following points:

● the people who heard Jesus could not read;
● these short sayings could be remembered easily;
● the church still learns and remembers these beatitudes;
● they remind people that life now is not everything;
● we must live our lives remembering God's laws.

ACTIVITIES

- Make a decorated set of the beatitudes to hang at home.
- Practise reading or reciting the beatitudes as choral speech. You could learn them by heart.
- Think of a common proverb and make up a play to show its meaning.
- Make an illustrated book of common proverbs.

DISPLAY

- Today's theme is the beatitudes.
- We learnt the beatitudes by heart.
- The beatitudes are like proverbs.
- Proverbs teach in a short form.
- Our work today is about proverbs.

EXPLORING WITH ADULTS

EXPERIENCE

- What proverbs and other well-known phrases and sayings stick in your mind?
- Why are proverbs and other sayings so memorable?
- How memorable are the beatitudes?

GOSPEL

- What do these sayings tell us about Jesus the teacher?
- How do you interpret these sayings for today?
- What do you understand by those addressed as poor and hungry?

APPLICATION

- How can the church draw attention to the beatitudes?
- How can you draw attention to the beatitudes?
- Can new beatitudes be written for today's liturgy?

CELEBRATING TOGETHER

WELCOMING CHILDREN

At an appropriate point in the service, invite the children to present their work on proverbs. If they have prepared some proverbs or sayings as choral speech, invite them to share these with the congregation. Develop a responsorial prayer around the theme of 'Blessed are …'.

HYMNS AND SONGS

Come and Praise
  4 Autumn days when the grass is jewelled
113 To ev'rything, turn, turn, turn

Hymns Ancient and Modern New Standard
238 Blest are the pure in heart
490 Lord, I have made thy word my choice

37
TEDDY BEARS

PREPARATION

GOSPEL THEME

The way of love (Matthew 5.38–48)

In the Sermon on the Mount, Jesus continues to compare and to contrast the teaching of the old law with the teaching of the new law. While the old law was concerned with justice, the new law is concerned with love. According to Jesus' teaching, his followers are required to love not only their friends, but their enemies as well.

We can begin to experience the significance of Matthew's teaching on the way of love by exploring our own love for our teddy bear and the teddy bear's uncompromising love for us.

AIMS

- to build on our present or previous love for our teddy bear;
- to extend our understanding of the teddy bear as a sign of love and acceptance;
- to respond to Jesus' invitation to love others.

EXPLORING WITH CHILDREN

STARTING

Bring in a well-loved teddy bear. Discuss it with the children, drawing out ideas of:

- teddy bears the children had or have;
- the most loved teddy bear they have seen;
- the love we feel for our teddy bears;
- the way we feel loved by our teddy bears;
- how we felt or feel when we hugged our teddy bears.

TALKING POINTS

Tell Jesus' words about love from Matthew. As you work, talk with the children about the significance of these. You could include the following points:

- Jesus spoke to a large crowd;
- they knew God's laws;
- they knew that God expected people to act with justice;
- Jesus said that justice is not enough;
- Jesus said we must love our enemies.

ACTIVITIES

- Draw a large outline of a teddy bear. Inside it write or draw loving words and actions.
- Make thank-you cards and notes to give to your teddy bears, thanking them for all the love they have given.
- Make teddy bear finger puppets or glove puppets.
- Make up your own plays about Jesus' words. You could have contrasting plays, one showing justice and one showing love.

DISPLAY

- Today's theme is the way of love.
- Jesus said love was more important than justice.
- Jesus taught us to love others.
- We feel loved by our teddy bears.
- Our work today is about teddy bears.

EXPLORING WITH ADULTS

EXPERIENCE

- What are your experiences of teddy bears?
- How did you feel about your teddy bear as a child?
- What stories do you have about your teddy bear?

GOSPEL

- What does this gospel say about the way of love?
- How do you interpret this message for today?
- How practical is Matthew's vision of the way of love?

APPLICATION

- How should the church demonstrate the way of love today?
- How should you live the way of love today?
- How should the way of love be proclaimed in liturgy?

CELEBRATING TOGETHER

WELCOMING CHILDREN

At an appropriate point in the service, invite the children to present their work on teddy bears. If members of the congregation have stories to share about their own teddy bears, invite them to do so.

HYMNS AND SONGS

Come and Praise
   10 God who made the earth
   27 There's a child in the streets

Hymns Ancient and Modern New Standard
   156 Come down, O Love divine
   365 God is love: let heav'n adore him

38 DOCTORS

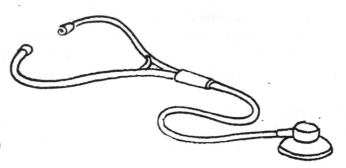

PREPARATION

GOSPEL THEME

The paralysed man (Mark 2.1–12)

In Mark's gospel, after Jesus has called the first four disciples he moves directly on to performing four major acts of healing. The case of the paralysed man is the fourth of these healings. On this occasion the paralysed man is lowered through the roof by four friends. Jesus says to the paralysed man 'Your sins are forgiven'. Mark is concerned to show that sickness, like sin, is a corruption of God's intentions for the perfect creation.

We can further deepen our understanding of Mark's message about Jesus the healer by exploring our own perceptions of doctors.

AIMS

- to build on our experiences of doctors;
- to see how doctors treat the whole person, not simply the sickness;
- to recognize Jesus the healer as restoring God's creation.

EXPLORING WITH CHILDREN

STARTING

Invite a doctor to come in, with his or her medical bag, or show a picture of a doctor or some medicine that a doctor has prescribed. Discuss the work of doctors, drawing out ideas of:

- the names of local doctors;
- times the children have been to a doctor;
- what the doctor did to help;
- things the doctor knows about us;
- doctors need to know about us to treat us.

TALKING POINTS

Tell the story from Mark of the paralysed man. As you work, talk with the children about the significance of Jesus the healer. You could include the following points:

- Jesus healed the man and he could walk;
- Jesus told him his sins were forgiven;
- Jesus healed the man of illness and sin;
- God did not intend illness or sin when he made the world;
- Jesus helps the world to be the way God created it.

ACTIVITIES

- Make doctors' coats out of white paper.
- Make stethoscopes or other items of medical equipment.
- Write an acrostic based on the words JESUS THE HEALER.
- Together write and draw a picture story book about Jesus healing the paralysed man. Each child could make a different section of the story.

DISPLAY

- Today's theme is the paralysed man.
- Jesus healed the paralysed man of illness and sin.
- Jesus wants the world to be well.
- Doctors treat people, not illnesses.
- Our work today is about doctors.

EXPLORING WITH ADULTS

EXPERIENCE

- What are your experiences of doctors?
- How do doctors relate to the whole person, not only the sickness?
- How is Jesus like and unlike a doctor?

GOSPEL

- What does this gospel say about Jesus' power over paralysis?
- How do you interpret this message for today?
- What do you understand by Jesus saying 'Your sins are forgiven'?

APPLICATION

- How should the church talk about the link between forgiveness and healing?
- How should you link forgiveness and healing?
- What is the place for forgiveness of sins in healing services today?

CELEBRATING TOGETHER

WELCOMING CHILDREN

At an appropriate point in the service, invite the children to present their work on doctors. If there are doctors in the congregation, invite them to lead part of the service. If the children have made stethoscopes, suggest that they wear them while the doctors lead the service.

HYMNS AND SONGS

Come and Praise
26 There is singing in the desert
68 Kum ba yah, my Lord

Hymns Ancient and Modern New Standard
133 Immortal Love for ever full
408 O God, whose will is life and good

39
BRIDGE BUILDERS

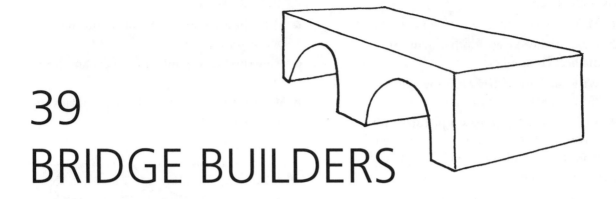

PREPARATION

GOSPEL THEME

The better way (Luke 6.27–38)

In the Sermon on the Plain, immediately after the beatitudes and woes, Luke presents a sequence of teaching on the Christian way of life. Followers of Jesus are to love their enemies, do good, and lend, expecting nothing in return. Above all, followers of Jesus are to be a forgiving people. They are to build bridges and not barriers.

We can begin to experience the significance of Jesus' teaching on the Christian way of life by exploring our understanding of bridges and the task of bridge builders.

AIMS

- to build on our experiences of bridges and bridge builders;
- to understand the Christian vocation as building bridges;
- to respond to Jesus' call to be bridge builders.

EXPLORING WITH CHILDREN

STARTING

Bring in a picture of a well-known bridge or a bridge made out of construction material such as Lego. Discuss bridges, drawing out ideas of:

- bridges the children have used;
- different types of bridges, such as footbridges;
- why we need bridges;
- the time and difficulty saved by using bridges;
- bridges are used to keep people together.

TALKING POINTS

Give a summary of Jesus' message from Luke. As you work, talk with the children about the significance of love and forgiveness. You could include the following points:

- anyone can love and help friends;
- Jesus said that Christians are to love enemies;
- Christians are to give to people who need help;
- Christians are to forgive;
- this means reaching out to other people, like crossing a bridge.

ACTIVITIES

- Make models of bridges from cardboard or from construction toys.
- Prepare a dance or drama showing people in need and Christians reaching out to help them.
- Prepare a poster with pictures of people in need on one side and pictures of yourselves crossing a bridge to help them.
- Use books to find out about some famous bridges, how they were built and who built them.

DISPLAY

- Today's theme is the better way
- Love is the better way.
- Christians are called to love, help and forgive.
- Bridge builders reach out to the other side.
- Our work today is about bridge builders.

EXPLORING WITH ADULTS

EXPERIENCE

- What are your experiences of bridges?
- How do bridges symbolize the Christian way of forgiveness?
- When have you been a bridge builder?

GOSPEL

- What does this gospel say about the Christian way of life?
- How do you interpret this message for today?
- What is the meaning of forgiveness?

APPLICATION

- How should the church proclaim forgiveness today?
- How should you proclaim forgiveness today?
- How should forgiveness be acknowledged in liturgy?

CELEBRATING TOGETHER

WELCOMING CHILDREN

At an appropriate point in the service, invite the children to present their work on bridge builders. If they have prepared a dance or drama on this theme, invite them to share it with the congregation.

HYMNS AND SONGS

Come and Praise
 55 Colours of day dawn into the mind
 61 All over the world

Hymns Ancient and Modern New Standard
 362 'Forgive our sins as we forgive'
 528 Where love and loving-kindness dwell

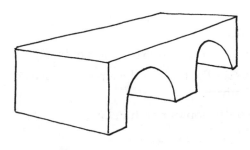

40
BIRDS

PREPARATION

GOSPEL THEME

The way of faith (Matthew 6.25–34)

In the Sermon on the Mount Jesus advocates the way of faith. In two important images, Jesus invites his listeners to learn from the birds of the air and from the lilies of the field. In contrast with men and women, the birds seem to live uncomplicated lives, and yet God takes care of them. We should learn from their example and put our faith in God.

We can begin to experience the significance of Matthew's teaching on the way of faith by exploring our own perceptions of the birds of the air.

AIMS

- to build on our experiences of birds;
- to see the birds of the air as exemplars of faith;
- to develop our faith in God.

EXPLORING WITH CHILDREN

STARTING

Bring in some bird seed or a book about birds. Discuss birds, drawing out ideas of:

- birds the children see in the local area;
- the feathers that keep birds warm;
- what birds use for nests;
- what birds eat;
- the things that birds need are freely available.

TALKING POINTS

Tell Jesus' words from Matthew about the birds. As you work, talk with the children about the significance of faith. You could include the following points:

- sometimes we worry a lot about food and clothes;
- Jesus said not to worry;
- life is more than food and drink and clothes;
- birds do not worry and they have enough to eat;
- God feeds birds and we are more valuable than birds.

ACTIVITIES

- Fold origami birds. (The local library should have origami books.)
- Prepare a dance on bird flight.
- Make bird-shaped badges with the message 'Trust God'.
- Bake biscuits in the shape of birds.

DISPLAY

- Today's theme is the way of faith.
- Jesus said not to worry.
- We can have faith in God.
- God takes care of the birds.
- Our work today is about birds.

EXPLORING WITH ADULTS

EXPERIENCE

- What are your experiences of birds?
- What do you find interesting about birds?
- What do you think of birds as exemplars of faith in God?

GOSPEL

- What does this gospel say about the way of faith?
- How do you interpret this message for today?
- Can life really be lived like this?

APPLICATION

- How should the church demonstrate the way of faith today?
- How should you live the way of faith today?
- How should the way of faith be proclaimed in liturgy?

CELEBRATING TOGETHER

WELCOMING CHILDREN

At an appropriate point in the service, invite the children to present their work on birds. If they have prepared a dance on bird flight, this can be presented, following the proclamation 'Look at the birds of the air'.

HYMNS AND SONGS

Come and Praise
  12 Who put the colours in the rainbow?
  15 There are hundreds of sparrows

Hymns Ancient and Modern New Standard
200 Fill thou my life, O Lord my God
436 Awake, our souls; away, our fears

41
WORDS

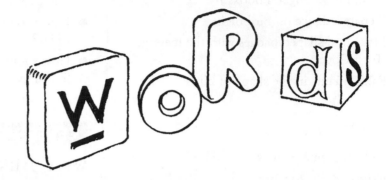

GOSPEL THEME

The divine word (John 1.1–14)

The first fourteen verses of John's gospel are generally known as the Prologue. Here John introduces themes which are central to his understanding of the person of Jesus. In the first sentence John uses the Greek word *logos* which is generally translated as 'word'. In fact the Greek word conveys much more than the simple translation suggests. The Greek word points to God's creative power, purpose and wisdom, and to the reason and rationality underpinning life.

We can begin to experience the significance of John's teaching about the *logos* by exploring our own perceptions of the power of words.

AIMS

● to build on our experiences and ideas of words;
● to appreciate the biblical image of Jesus as the Word;
● to experience the significance of *logos* in John's gospel.

EXPLORING WITH CHILDREN

STARTING

Bring in a book containing some words or a saying that has meant a lot to you. Read it. Discuss the power of words, drawing out ideas of:

● words that stick in children's minds, including adverts;
● feelings they associate with these words;
● words that make them happy, such as 'well done';
● words that upset them;
● words that inspire them to be creative.

TALKING POINTS

Tell John's account of Jesus as the Word. As you work, talk with the children about the significance of this. You could include the following points:

● Jesus is described as the Word;
● Jesus the Word created the world;
● Jesus the Word brought life and light to all;
● Jesus is the Word made human.

ACTIVITIES

- Make banners or posters of words which inspire you, or of words such as 'Jesus is the Word of life'.
- Look through dictionaries, each person choosing a different letter, and make lists of words that make you happy, words that upset you, and words that inspire you.
- Make up an acrostic about Jesus, using as your base JESUS or WORD or LOGOS.
- Play a miming game. One person chooses a word or phrase to mime and the rest try to guess what it is.

DISPLAY

- Today's theme is the divine word.
- Jesus is the Word.
- Words are very powerful.
- We chose words that mean a lot to us.
- Our work today is about words.

EXPLORING WITH ADULTS

EXPERIENCE

- What stories can you tell about the power of words?
- How can words actually change people and things?
- How do you understand Jesus as the Word?

GOSPEL

- What does the gospel tell us about Jesus as the Word?
- How do you interpret John's message about the Word for today?
- How do you understand the relationship between the Word and God?

APPLICATION

- How should the church present Jesus as the Word today?
- How should the image of Jesus as the Word influence your personal spirituality?
- How should the image of Jesus as the Word be used in liturgy?

CELEBRATING TOGETHER

WELCOMING CHILDREN

At an appropriate point in the service, invite the children to present their work on words. If they have produced banners or posters about words, these can be held high during the gospel reading.

HYMNS AND SONGS

Come and Praise
  5 Carpenter, carpenter, make me a tree
 72 Ev'ry word comes alive

Hymns Ancient and Modern New Standard
 132 Son of God, eternal Saviour
 250 Thou didst leave thy throne and thy kingly crown

42 STORMS

PREPARATION

GOSPEL THEME

Jesus stills the storm (Luke 8.22–25)

The gospel writers demonstrate Jesus' power over the forces of evil and chaos. Jesus drives out demons and cures the possessed. In the present narrative Jesus is doing more than simply calming a storm at sea. In this narrative Jesus is engaging with the primordial forces of chaos, just as God overcame the forces of the storm in the original act of creation. No wonder that the disciples were afraid and amazed.

We can begin to experience the significance of Luke's teaching about the stilling of the storm by exploring our own experiences of the power of storms and their potential to be destructive.

AIMS

- to build on our experiences and ideas of storms;
- to understand the biblical image of the storm;
- to see Jesus' power over the storm as a sign of God's Kingdom.

EXPLORING WITH CHILDREN

STARTING

Bring in a raincoat or a picture of a stormy sky. Discuss storms, drawing out ideas of:

- storms the children have experienced;
- storms they have seen on television;
- the power of storms to destroy and to create chaos;
- their feelings during a storm;
- their feelings when the storm ends.

TALKING POINTS

Tell the story from Luke of the storm. As you work, talk with the children about the significance of Jesus' action. You could include the following points:

- the disciples knew the storm was dangerous;
- they were afraid;
- Jesus had power to calm the storm and create peace;
- this was like God's power in creating the world;
- this was a sign of Jesus as God's Son.

ACTIVITIES

- Paint pictures of stormy seas or do finger-paintings of waves.
- Fill a tub or baby's bath with water. Add plastic boats. Blow through straws to create a stormy sea.
- Compose music or prepare a dance or mime about the storm and its dramatic stilling.
- Write an imaginary newspaper report of the storm.

DISPLAY

- Today's theme is Jesus stilling the storm.
- Jesus had power over the storm.
- Jesus brought peace to the disciples.
- We thought about the power of storms.
- Our work today is about storms.

EXPLORING WITH ADULTS

EXPERIENCE

- What are your experiences of storms?
- How do you interpret the power of storms?
- How does the storm become a sign of chaos and evil?

GOSPEL

- What does the gospel tell us about Jesus' power over the storm?
- How do you interpret this message for today?
- How do you understand the stilling of the storm?

APPLICATION

- How should the church present the stilling of the storm today?
- How should you apply this story to your own life?
- How should the image of storms be used in preaching today?

CELEBRATING TOGETHER

WELCOMING CHILDREN

At an appropriate point in the service, invite the children to present their work on storms. If they have prepared dance, mime or music showing the gathering storm and the dramatic stilling, this can be presented immediately before the gospel reading.

HYMNS AND SONGS

Come and Praise
6 The earth is yours, O God
78 By brother sun who brings the day

Hymns Ancient and Modern New Standard
132 Son of God, eternal Saviour
232 Lord, be thy word my rule

43 MOUNTAIN

PREPARATION

GOSPEL THEME

Transfiguration (Matthew 17.1–9)

The season of Epiphany is concerned with the theme of revelation, how the presence and power of God is made known through the person of Jesus. On the first Sunday after Epiphany the voice from heaven proclaimed 'This is my Son' at Jesus' baptism. On the last Sunday after Epiphany the same voice speaks at Jesus' transfiguration. This time the divine revelation takes place, appropriately, on a high mountain, where heaven and earth meet.

We can begin to experience the significance of Matthew's teaching on the transfiguration by exploring our own perceptions of the mystery and awesome nature of mountains.

AIMS

- to build on our experiences and images of mountains;
- to feel the awe-inspiring majesty of mountains;
- to enter into the experience of the transfiguration.

EXPLORING WITH CHILDREN

STARTING

Bring in a picture, photograph or model of a mountain. Discuss mountains, drawing out ideas of:

- mountains the children can name;
- any mountains they have seen;
- the highest mountains;
- the way mountains appear to meet the sky;
- how we feel when we gaze at mountains.

TALKING POINTS

Tell the story from Matthew of the transfiguration. As you work, talk with the children about the significance of this. You could include the following points:

- Jesus was changed;
- Moses and Elijah appeared suddenly;
- a voice from heaven claimed Jesus as 'my Son';
- the same voice had spoken at Jesus' baptism;
- the transfiguration showed the power of God in Jesus.

ACTIVITIES

- Build a mountain from papier mâché.
- Pretend to climb a high mountain. Make cardboard replicas of equipment you will need. Tie yourselves together with string or rope. Struggle up to the top.
- Imagine you had been on the mountain with Jesus. Paint or write or dance your feelings.
- Paint a mural for the wall, showing the mountain and all those on it.

DISPLAY

- Today's theme is the transfiguration.
- God was present in Jesus.
- God called Jesus 'my Son'.
- Jesus was transfigured on the mountain.
- Our work today is about mountains.

EXPLORING WITH ADULTS

EXPERIENCE

- What are your experiences of mountains?
- How do high and awesome mountains make you feel?
- Why did the transfiguration take place on a high mountain?

GOSPEL

- What does this gospel say about Jesus?
- How do you interpret this message for today?
- What is the significance of Peter, James and John?

APPLICATION

- How should the church proclaim Jesus' transfiguration today?
- How should you witness to Jesus' transfiguration today?
- How can the image of high mountains be used in liturgy?

CELEBRATING TOGETHER

WELCOMING CHILDREN

At an appropriate point in the service, invite the children to present their work on mountains. Obtain slides of mountains and project these while appropriate awesome music is played.

HYMNS AND SONGS

Come and Praise
  1 Morning has broken
 36 God is love

Hymns Ancient and Modern New Standard
318 'Tis good, Lord, to be here
441 Christ upon the mountain peak

44
PURE WHITE

PREPARATION

GOSPEL THEME

Transfiguration (Mark 9.2–9)

The season of Epiphany is concerned with the theme of revelation, how the presence and power of God is made known through the person of Jesus. On the first Sunday after Epiphany the voice from heaven proclaimed 'You are my Son' at Jesus' baptism. On the last Sunday after Epiphany the same voice speaks at Jesus' transfiguration. This time the divine revelation clothes Jesus, appropriately, with robes of pure and dazzling white.

We can begin to experience the significance of Mark's teaching on the transfiguration by exploring our own perceptions of the mystery and awesome nature of pure white.

AIMS

- to build on our experiences and images of pure white;
- to feel the awe-inspiring majesty of pure white;
- to enter into the experience of the transfiguration.

EXPLORING WITH CHILDREN

STARTING

Bring in a sheet of white paper or cardboard. At some stage, add a faint dirty mark to it. Focus on the white, drawing out ideas of:

- how clean it looks;
- the way the slightest speck of dirt shows up;
- things the children own or see that are pure white;
- good things they think of when they look at white;
- white can be very dazzling and awesome.

TALKING POINTS

Tell the story from Mark of the transfiguration. As you work, talk with the children about the significance of this. You could include the following points:

- Jesus was changed;
- his clothes became pure white;
- Moses and Elijah appeared suddenly;
- a voice from heaven claimed Jesus as 'my Son';
- the transfiguration showed the power of God.

ACTIVITIES

- If you know how to produce colours from white light through a prism, do so. Another way is to place a mirror at an angle in a basin of water and shine a light onto it.
- Paint white pictures on dark paper, or use white crayons or pencils.
- Bleach some dirty white rags to see the difference it makes. (Handle the bleach carefully.)
- Interview 'Peter', 'James' and 'John' about their experience.

DISPLAY

- Today's theme is the transfiguration.
- God called Jesus 'my Son'.
- The transfiguration showed God's power.
- Jesus' clothes were changed to pure white.
- Our work today is about pure white.

EXPLORING WITH ADULTS

EXPERIENCE

- What are your experiences of pure whiteness?
- How does pure white make you feel?
- Why did Jesus' clothes become dazzling white?

GOSPEL

- What does this gospel say about Jesus?
- How do you interpret this message for today?
- What is the significance of Moses and Elijah?

APPLICATION

- How should the church proclaim Jesus' transfiguration today?
- How should you witness to Jesus' transfiguration today?
- How can the image of pure white be used in liturgy?

CELEBRATING TOGETHER

WELCOMING CHILDREN

At an appropriate point in the service, invite the children to present their work on pure white. Produce a large sheet of pure white glossy card and invite the congregation to focus attention on this card while appropriate awesome music is played.

HYMNS AND SONGS

Come and Praise
   7 All creatures of our God and King
147 Make me a channel of your peace

Hymns Ancient and Modern New Standard
131 Love divine, all loves excelling
346 Christ is the world's true light

45
WHITE CLOUDS

PREPARATION

GOSPEL THEME

Transfiguration (Luke 9.28–36)

The season of Epiphany is concerned with the theme of revelation, how the presence and power of God is made known through the person of Jesus. On the first Sunday after Epiphany the voice from heaven proclaimed 'You are my Son' at Jesus' baptism. On the last Sunday after Epiphany the same voice speaks at Jesus' transfiguration. This time the divine revelation envelops Jesus, appropriately in a cloud. This cloud is an image for the divine glory.

We can begin to experience the significance of Luke's teaching on the transfiguration by exploring our own perceptions of the mystery and awesome nature of white clouds in a clear sky.

AIMS

- to build on our experiences and images of clouds;
- to feel the awe-inspiring majesty of clouds;
- to enter into the experience of the transfiguration.

EXPLORING WITH CHILDREN

STARTING

Go out to look at the clouds. Discuss these, drawing out ideas of:

- different types of clouds;
- any favourite types the children have;
- what clouds actually are;
- what clouds tell us about the weather;
- times the children have been in mist, low-lying clouds.

TALKING POINTS

Tell the story from Luke of the transfiguration. As you work, talk with the children about the significance of this. You could include the following points:

- Jesus was changed;
- Moses and Elijah appeared suddenly;
- a cloud came and hid them all;
- a voice from the cloud called Jesus 'my Son';
- the transfiguration showed the power of God in Jesus.

ACTIVITIES

- Cut out and colour large models of clouds to display in the church, or draw or paint some of the clouds you can see outside.
- Make an edible picture of clouds, with marzipan or icing clouds on a background of blue icing.
- Research the nature of clouds and draw up a chart showing different types of clouds and the weather associated with each.
- Create music about the transfiguration. Discuss the feelings involved in each part of the story and assign each of those feelings to a small group to express with their instruments.

DISPLAY

- Today's theme is the transfiguration.
- A voice from the cloud called Jesus 'my Son'.
- The transfiguration showed God's power.
- We studied and drew clouds.
- Our work today is about white clouds.

EXPLORING WITH ADULTS

EXPERIENCE

- What are your experiences of white clouds in a clear sky?
- How do white clouds in a clear sky make you feel?
- Why did the transfiguration include the cloud?

GOSPEL

- What does this gospel say about Jesus?

- How do you interpret this message for today?
- How did the disciples feel?

APPLICATION

- How should the church proclaim Jesus' transfiguration today?
- How should you witness to Jesus' transfiguration today?
- How can the church's liturgy express Jesus' transfiguration?

CELEBRATING TOGETHER

WELCOMING CHILDREN

At an appropriate point in the service, invite the children to present their work on white clouds. If the children have made large cut-out clouds, these can be hoisted high above the congregation.

HYMNS AND SONGS

Come and Praise
  30 Join with us
  89 Guess how I feel

Hymns Ancient and Modern New Standard
    4 Christ, whose glory fills the skies
  502 O raise your eyes on high and see

Introduction to the Season of Lent

Traditionally for the church the season of Lent is a sombre period of fasting and preparation. Through fasting the people of God prepare themselves for the events of Holy Week, the betrayal, crucifixion and death of Jesus. The traditional themes of Lent include temptation, repentance and renewed dedication.

The gospel readings for the first Sunday of Lent focus on the temptations of Jesus in the wilderness. The significance of this theme at the beginning of Lent is concerned not with encouraging children to resist temptations but with helping them to explore the models of Messiahship which Jesus rejected. The project activities see three rejected models in terms of magician, stunt man and pop star.

In contrast with the first Sunday of Lent, the gospel readings for the second Sunday of Lent focus on the model of Messiahship which Jesus embraced, the model which led inevitably to the cross. The project activities explore three powerful images of the cross: the Christus Rex of Jesus reigning from the cross, the classic crucifix of Jesus nailed to the cross, and the empty cross.

The gospel readings for the third Sunday of Lent select three images of the new beginning which is offered to the people of God through the death and resurrection of Jesus. The project activities develop these images by exploring the ideas of living water, spring cleaning and gardening.

The fourth Sunday of Lent is generally kept as Mothering Sunday and seen as a period of refreshment during the middle of Lent. The two gospel readings illustrate the relationship between Jesus and Mary his mother. The project activities concentrate on Mary the archetypal mother rather than on the children's own mothers for two reasons: to develop knowledge of the scriptural tradition and to respect the fluidity in contemporary patterns of family life.

The gospel readings for the fifth Sunday of Lent anticipate the death of Jesus and foreshadow the resurrection. The project activities help the children to face the news of Good Friday in the context of the Christian hope.

The last Sunday of Lent introduces the events of Holy Week by celebrating Jesus' triumphal entry into Jerusalem when the crowds tore branches from the trees. The project activities help children to enter into the pageantry of Palm Sunday by concentrating on making processional banners, processional crosses and processional robes.

46
THE MAGICIAN

PREPARATION

GOSPEL THEME

Temptations in the wilderness (Matthew 4.1–11)

All three synoptic gospels portray Jesus' ministry by beginning with a period of forty days in the wilderness tempted by Satan. Both Matthew and Luke describe three of the temptations experienced. Each of these three temptations challenges Jesus to adopt a model of Messiahship which would win power and wide public appeal, and not lead to the inevitable cross on Good Friday. Matthew and Luke agree in placing first the temptation to turn stones into bread. A Messiah who could turn stones into bread would be guaranteed a following.

We can begin to experience the kind of Messiahship which Jesus rejected by exploring our images of the magician.

AIMS

- to build on our experiences of magicians;
- to help us understand the kind of following the magician attracts;
- to see the kind of Messiahship Jesus rejected.

EXPLORING WITH CHILDREN

STARTING

Bring in a magic trick or a picture of a magician. Discuss magicians, drawing out ideas of:

- magicians the children have seen on television or stage;
- magicians in books;
- the power of story book magicians;
- magic tricks they know or have seen;
- how they would feel if magicians were real.

TALKING POINTS

Tell the story from Matthew of Jesus' temptations. As you work, talk with the children about the significance of Jesus' choice. You could include the following points:

- the devil wanted Jesus to perform tricks like a magician;
- people would have been impressed by the tricks;
- people would have followed Jesus to see more tricks;
- Jesus wanted to serve people, not to amaze them;
- Jesus refused the temptation to be famous.

ACTIVITIES

- Make magicians' clothes and props.
- Rehearse some magic tricks. Your local library should give ideas.
- Prepare an imaginary interview with some-one who has seen Jesus turn stones into bread. Include questions about what they want to see Jesus do next and how they will feel if he does not 'perform' well.
- Make posters headed 'Jesus said No!' (about turning stones into bread just to show off) and 'Jesus said Yes!' (about feeding hungry people when they needed help).

DISPLAY

- Today's theme is the temptations in the wilderness.
- The devil tempted Jesus to show off.
- Jesus chose to obey God.
- Jesus was tempted to act like a magician.
- Our work today is about magicians.

EXPLORING WITH ADULTS

EXPERIENCE

- What are your experiences of magicians?
- Why are people so fascinated by magicians?
- How useful is the image of the magician as a model of false power?

GOSPEL

- What does this gospel say about the temp-tation to turn stones into bread?
- How do you interpret this message for today?
- What do you understand by the temptation to turn stones into bread?

APPLICATION

- Does the church face a similar temptation today?
- Do you face a similar temptation today?
- How can this theme best be communicated in liturgy?

CELEBRATING TOGETHER

WELCOMING CHILDREN

At an appropriate point in the service, invite the children to present their work on the magician. If they have rehearsed any magic tricks, invite them to display these tricks immediately before the gospel reading.

HYMNS AND SONGS

Come and Praise
7 All creatures of our God and King
90 I come like a beggar with a gift in my hand

Hymns Ancient and Modern New Standard
56 Forty days and forty nights
136 Jesus, grant me this, I pray

47
THE STUNTMAN

PREPARATION

GOSPEL THEME

Temptations in the wilderness (Mark 1.9–15)

All three synoptic gospels portray Jesus' ministry beginning with a period of forty days in the wilderness tempted by Satan. Unlike Matthew and Luke, Mark's account does not describe the temptations experienced by Jesus. The temptations described by Matthew and Luke challenge Jesus to adopt a model of Messiahship which would win power and wide public appeal, and not lead to the inevitable cross on Good Friday. In one of these temptations Jesus is challenged to throw himself from the pinnacle of the temple. A Messiah who could survive such activities would be guaranteed a following.

We can begin to experience the kind of Messiahship which Jesus rejected by exploring our images of the stuntman.

AIMS

● to build on our experiences of stuntmen;
● to help us understand the kind of following the stuntman attracts;
● to see the kind of Messiahship Jesus rejected.

EXPLORING WITH CHILDREN

STARTING

Bring in a magazine article about the work of a stuntman, or a picture showing an incredible stunt. Discuss these, drawing out ideas of:

● stunts the children have seen on television or stage;
● stunts the children have read about;
● stunts they have tried for themselves;
● the crowds who watch 'daredevil' stunts;
● their own feelings about stuntmen.

TALKING POINTS

Tell the story from Mark of Jesus' temptations, reminding the children of the temptation for Jesus to throw himself from the temple. As you work, talk with the children about the significance of Jesus' choice. You could include the following points:

● the devil wanted Jesus to perform tricks like a stuntman;
● people would have been impressed by the stunts;
● people would have followed Jesus to see more stunts;
● Jesus wanted to serve people, not to amaze them;
● Jesus refused the temptation to be famous.

ACTIVITIES

- Watch a video about the work of stuntmen or show extracts of dangerous stunts from various television programmes.
- Prepare your own comic stunt show, using toy animals, sound effects and a good descriptive commentary.
- Prepare a dance of people whirling around Jesus, 'tempting' him by pretending to offer various things.
- Construct a model of the temple (from cardboard, Lego, blocks, etc.) with a figure on top representing the temptation, and figures below showing Jesus' choice to serve people rather than to amaze them.

DISPLAY

- Today's theme is the temptations in the wilderness.
- The devil tempted Jesus to show off.
- Jesus chose to serve God.
- Jesus was tempted to act like a stuntman.
- Our work today is about stuntmen.

EXPLORING WITH ADULTS

EXPERIENCE

- What are your experiences of stuntmen?
- Why are people so fascinated by stuntmen?
- How useful is the image of the stuntman as a model of false power?

GOSPEL

- What do Matthew and Luke say about the temptation to jump from the temple?
- How do you interpret this message for today?

- What do you understand by the temptation to jump from the temple?

APPLICATION

- Does the church face a similar temptation today?
- Do you face a similar temptation today?
- How can this theme best be communicated in liturgy?

CELEBRATING TOGETHER

WELCOMING CHILDREN

At an appropriate point in the service, invite the children to present their work on the stuntman. If a video has been obtained or made showing extracts of stuntmen at work, this can be shown immediately before the gospel reading.

HYMNS AND SONGS

Come and Praise
  13 O praise Him!
  48 Father, hear the prayer we offer

Hymns Ancient and Modern New Standard
   9 At even, ere the sun was set
224 Lead us, heavenly Father, lead us

48
THE POP STAR

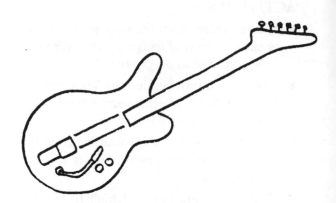

PREPARATION

GOSPEL THEME

Temptations in the wilderness (Luke 4.1–13)

All three synoptic gospels portray Jesus' ministry beginning with a period of forty days in the wilderness tempted by Satan. Both Matthew and Luke describe three of the temptations experienced. Each of these three temptations challenges Jesus to adopt a model of Messiahship which would win power and wide public appeal, and not lead to the inevitable cross on Good Friday. In the second of the temptations described by Luke (the third in Matthew's order), Jesus contemplates the opportunity of commanding worldly fame and power (i.e., the kingdom of the world).

We can begin to experience the kind of Messiahship which Jesus rejected by exploring our images of the international fame and power of pop stars.

AIMS

- to build on our experiences of pop stars;
- to help us understand the kind of following the pop star attracts;
- to see the kind of Messiahship Jesus rejected.

EXPLORING WITH CHILDREN

STARTING

Play a current pop song by a well-known pop star. Discuss this, drawing out ideas of:

- the children's favourite songs;
- the children's favourite pop stars;
- pop stars they have seen on stage or on television;
- the way the crowd reacts to pop stars;
- the power of pop stars.

TALKING POINTS

Tell the story from Luke of Jesus' temptations. As you work, talk with the children about the significance of Jesus' choice. You could include the following points:

- the devil wanted Jesus to worship him;
- in return the devil promised Jesus power;
- people would have followed and obeyed Jesus;
- Jesus chose to serve people, not to have power over them;
- Jesus refused the temptation to be powerful.

ACTIVITIES

- Make a book or display about a pop star, including biographical details, magazine photographs, lists of songs, etc.

- Write a review of your favourite pop star or design clothes for your favourite pop star to wear.

- Make double-sided masks on paper plates. On one side draw a glittering pop star. On the other side portray the caring, serving Jesus.

- Act out the temptations of Jesus.

DISPLAY

- Today's theme is the temptations in the wilderness.

- The devil tempted Jesus with power.

- Jesus chose to worship God.

- Jesus was tempted to act like a pop star.

- Our work today is about pop stars.

EXPLORING WITH ADULTS

EXPERIENCE

- What is your experience of pop stars?

- Why are people so fascinated by pop stars?

- How useful is the image of the pop star as a model of future power?

GOSPEL

- What does this gospel say about the temptation to gain the kingdoms of the world?

- How do you interpret this message for today?

- What do you understand by the temptation to gain the kingdoms of the world?

APPLICATION

- Does the church face a similar temptation today?

- Do you face a similar temptation today?

- How can this theme best be communicated in liturgy?

CELEBRATING TOGETHER

WELCOMING CHILDREN

At an appropriate point in the service, invite the children to present their work on the pop star. If they have profiled a particular pop star, play a recording of this pop star immediately before the gospel reading.

HYMNS AND SONGS

Come and Praise
  41 Fill thou my life
  39 O Lord, all the world belongs to you

Hymns Ancient and Modern New Standard
129 Lord Jesus, think on me
436 Awake, our souls; away, our fears

49
CHRISTUS REX

PREPARATION

GOSPEL THEME

Prediction of the passion to Nicodemus
(John 3.1–17)

As is usual in John's gospel, a number of major themes are compressed into this encounter between Jesus and Nicodemus. The theme of significance for the second Sunday of Lent concerns the covert prediction of Jesus' death on the cross. This prediction draws on the story in Numbers 21.4–9. When Moses lifted up the serpent, those who looked at it were preserved in life. In a similar way Jesus will be lifted up on the cross and thereby bring life to those who believe in him.

We can begin to experience the significance of John's message concerning the crucifixion by exploring our own reactions to the Christus Rex, the image of Christ reigning from the cross.

AIMS

● to build on our experiences of the Christus Rex;
● to help us understand the healing power of the cross;
● to see Jesus lifted up and reigning from the cross.

EXPLORING WITH CHILDREN

STARTING

Bring in a Christus Rex, an image of Jesus reigning from the cross. Discuss this, drawing out ideas of:

● the difference between this and other crosses;
● any images the children have seen like this;
● any such images you have in your own church building;
● the Latin word *rex* means 'king';
● we call Jesus King.

TALKING POINTS

Tell the story from John of Nicodemus meeting Jesus. As you work, talk with the children about the significance of Jesus' prediction. You could include the following points:

● Jesus predicted that he would be 'lifted up';
● this happened on the cross;
● his death on the cross brought life to those who believe;
● Jesus' cross is like the throne of a king;
● Jesus chose to die for us instead of acting like a magician.

ACTIVITIES

- Make your own image or painting of a Christus Rex. You may like to put a crown around the outside of it to remind yourself of Jesus reigning.
- Compose music that makes you think of Jesus reigning.
- Draw twin pictures – of Moses lifting up the serpent to bring healing and Jesus being lifted on the cross to bring healing to the world.
- Look through the hymn-book to find hymns that speak of Jesus reigning or ruling.

DISPLAY

- Today's theme is the prediction of the passion to Nicodemus.
- Jesus told Nicodemus he would be lifted up.
- Jesus reigns from the cross.
- Jesus chose to die on a cross to heal the world.
- Our work today is about the Christus Rex.

EXPLORING WITH ADULTS

EXPERIENCE

- What are your experiences of the Christus Rex?
- How do you feel when you look at the Christus Rex?
- How helpful is the Christus Rex in personal devotion?

GOSPEL

- What does this gospel say about Jesus being lifted up?

- How do you interpret this message for today?
- What do you understand by the promise 'everyone who believes in him may have eternal life'?

APPLICATION

- How should the church respond to the Christus Rex today?
- How should you respond to the Christus Rex today?
- How should the church deploy the Christus Rex in liturgy?

CELEBRATING TOGETHER

WELCOMING CHILDREN

At an appropriate point in the service, invite the children to present their work on the Christus Rex. If slides have been obtained of the Christus Rex (say Graham Sutherland's well-known image from Coventry Cathedral), these should be projected immediately after the gospel reading.

HYMNS AND SONGS

Come and Praise
36 God is love, His the care
58 At the name of Jesus

Hymns Ancient and Modern New Standard
59 Sing, my tongue, the glorious battle
334 A man there lived in Galilee

50
THE CROSS

PREPARATION

GOSPEL THEME

Prediction of the passion to the disciples
(Mark 8.31–38)

In Mark's gospel Jesus begins to teach his disciples about his forthcoming crucifixion as soon as Peter has publicly acknowledged him as the Christ in the verses immediately preceding this passage. There are two other predictions of the crucifixion later in Mark's gospel, each becoming more explicit and precise. On this first occasion the disciples fail to understand and the crowds are invited to take up their cross and to follow him.

We can begin to experience the central place of the cross in the Christian tradition by exploring our own reactions to the simple cross without the figure of Jesus.

AIMS

● to build on our experiences of the cross;
● to help us understand the power of the cross in Christian symbolism;
● to hear Jesus' invitation to take up our cross and to follow him.

EXPLORING WITH CHILDREN

STARTING

Bring in an empty cross. Discuss it, drawing out ideas of:

● the difference between this and other crosses;
● any such crosses the children have seen, including jewellery;
● any such crosses you have in your own church building;
● what they think of when they see the empty cross;
● the empty cross is an important Christian symbol.

TALKING POINTS

Tell the story from Mark of Jesus' prediction. As you work, talk with the children about the significance of this. You could include the following points:

● Jesus told the disciples he would be killed and rise again;
● Peter told him off;
● Jesus invited the crowd to follow him and take up their cross;
● this means to live Jesus' way;
● Jesus chose to die for us instead of acting like a stuntman.

ACTIVITIES

- Make papier mâché models of the empty cross.
- Roll out pre-prepared biscuit dough and cut out biscuits in the shape of the empty cross.
- Make cross-shaped badges to wear and to give to others in the congregation.
- Cut out potato print blocks in the shape of a cross and use these to print a pattern of crosses in many colours for a wall display.

DISPLAY

- Today's theme is the prediction of the passion to the disciples.
- Jesus invited the crowd to take up their cross.
- Jesus predicted he would be killed and rise again.
- Jesus chose to die for us.
- Our work today is about the cross.

EXPLORING WITH ADULTS

EXPERIENCE

- What is your experience of the empty cross?
- How do you feel when you look at the empty cross?
- How helpful is the empty cross in personal devotion?

GOSPEL

- What does the gospel say about Jesus' death?
- How do you interpret this message for today?
- What do you understand by the invitation to 'take up their cross'?

APPLICATION

- How should the church respond to the empty cross today?
- How should you respond to the empty cross today?
- How should the church deploy the cross in liturgy?

CELEBRATING TOGETHER

WELCOMING CHILDREN

At an appropriate point in the service, invite the children to present their work on the empty cross. If small lapel badges of the cross have been made for members of the congregation to wear, these can be distributed and the people invited to wear them.

HYMNS AND SONGS

Come and Praise
  34 Praise to the Lord
147 Make me a channel of your peace

Hymns Ancient and Modern New Standard
  72 Lift high the Cross, the love of Christ proclaim
138 We sing the praise of him who died

51
CRUCIFIX

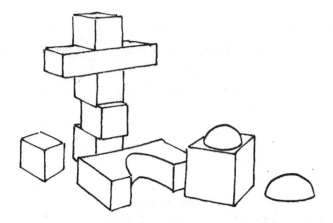

PREPARATION

GOSPEL THEME

Prediction of the passion in Jerusalem
(Luke 13.31–35)

In Luke's gospel, Jesus' journey to Jerusalem has particular power and poignancy as the place in which he will meet his death. In this passage Jesus sets his own impending death in the context of the prophets who have been killed in Jerusalem. There is also an elliptical reference to the third day on which Jesus finishes his work. The third day is the day of resurrection.

We can begin to experience the significance of the crucifixion in the Christian tradition by exploring our own reactions to the crucifix, the suffering Jesus nailed to the cross.

AIMS

- to build on our experiences of the crucifix;
- to help us understand the shape of Jesus' ministry leading to the cross;
- to travel with Jesus on the road to Jerusalem during Lent.

EXPLORING WITH CHILDREN

STARTING

Bring in a crucifix, with the suffering Jesus nailed to the cross. Discuss this, drawing out ideas of:

- the difference between this and other crosses;
- any other crucifixes the children have seen;
- any crucifixes you have in your own church building;
- what they think of when they see Jesus suffering on the cross;
- the crucifix is an important Christian symbol.

TALKING POINTS

Tell the story from Luke of Jesus predicting his passion. As you work, talk with the children about the significance of this. You could include the following points:

- Jesus knew he would be killed in Jerusalem;
- he knew he would suffer;
- he still loved Jerusalem and all its people;
- he continued to help people even though it would bring his death;
- he chose to die like this rather than to be famous like a pop star.

ACTIVITIES

- Make a display of different crucifixes. Add your own drawings if you wish.
- Paint, draw or write about some of the people Jesus healed. Arrange these along a roadway, for it was these that led Jesus to the cross.
- Pretend to be Jesus and the disciples walking along the road to Jerusalem. The 'disciples' question and 'Jesus' answers, giving reasons for his actions.
- Make a model of Jerusalem (from building blocks, cardboard, etc.) and the road leading to it. Place Jesus along the road, helping people in need.

DISPLAY

- Today's theme is the prediction of the passion in Jerusalem.
- Jesus predicted he would die in Jerusalem.
- Jesus' work led to the cross.
- Jesus chose to suffer and die for us.
- Our work today is about the crucifix.

EXPLORING WITH ADULTS

EXPERIENCE

- What is your experience of the crucifix?
- How do you feel when you look at the crucifix?
- How helpful is the crucifix in personal devotion?

GOSPEL

- What does the gospel say about Jesus' death?
- How do you interpret this message for today?

- What do you understand by the text 'on the third day I finish my work'?

APPLICATION

- How should the church respond to the crucifix today?
- How should you respond to the crucifix today?
- How should the church deploy the crucifix in liturgy?

CELEBRATING TOGETHER

WELCOMING CHILDREN

At an appropriate point in the service, invite the children to present their work on the crucifix. If a range of crucifixes has been assembled, these can be displayed during the gospel reading.

HYMNS AND SONGS

Come and Praise
- 10 God who made the earth
- 38 Now thank we all our God

Hymns Ancient and Modern New Standard
- 63 My song is love unknown
- 387 Lord Christ, when first thou cam'st to men

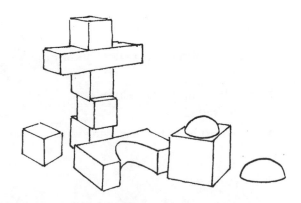

52 RUNNING WATER

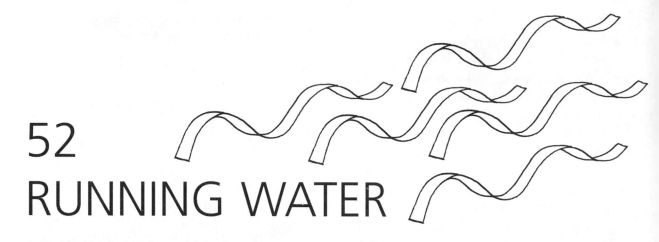

PREPARATION

GOSPEL THEME

Living water brings eternal life (John 4.5–42)

The image of water has already played an important part in John's gospel. Now the image is transformed in two ways. First, the image is now concerned with 'living water'. The flowing, moving, dynamic nature of living water is contrasted with the still, motionless water at the bottom of the well. Second, this living water, like Jesus himself, holds the key to eternal life. Here is one of the images of Messiahship held out during Lent.

We can begin to experience the significance of John's message about living water by exploring our own images of running water.

AIMS

- to build on our experiences of running water;
- to help us understand John's image of living water;
- to turn to Jesus for that living water.

EXPLORING WITH CHILDREN

STARTING

Bring in a picture of a waterfall. Discuss this, drawing out ideas of:

- famous waterfalls the children can name;
- waterfalls the children have seen;
- places we see running water, at home or outside;
- the beauty and power of running water;
- the liveliness or life of running water.

TALKING POINTS

Tell the story from John of Jesus meeting the Samaritan woman. As you work, talk with the children about the significance of living water. You could include the following points:

- Jesus promised living water;
- this living water is inside us;
- it gushes up like a spring and overflows like a waterfall;
- it leads us to eternal life;
- the living water is a picture of Jesus' life within us.

ACTIVITIES

- Make a model waterfall with tilted bowls and stones for effect. Add the water in the top and watch it run to the bottom. Compare the running, living water with the still water in your bowl at the bottom.
- Most children enjoy playing with water. Set up baby's baths and various shaped containers for pouring.
- Prepare a tape recording of the woman talking to Jesus. Prepare background noises of water being poured, running, etc.
- Write adverts for Jesus, the living water.

DISPLAY

- Today's theme is the living water that brings eternal life.
- Jesus promised living water.
- Jesus is the water of life.
- Running water is a symbol of life.
- Our work today is about running water.

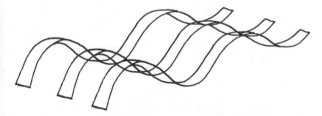

EXPLORING WITH ADULTS

EXPERIENCE

- What is your experience of running water?
- What are the properties of running water?
- Is running water a helpful image of Jesus' Messiahship?

GOSPEL

- What does this gospel say about living water?

- How do you interpret this message for today?
- What do you understand by living water?

APPLICATION

- How should the church proclaim the message of living water today?
- How should you proclaim the message of living water today?
- How should the image of living water be used in liturgy?

CELEBRATING TOGETHER

WELCOMING CHILDREN

At an appropriate point in the service, invite the children to present their work on running water. If a garden fountain is available, this can be set running in the church, or slides or pictures of waterfalls can be displayed during the gospel reading.

HYMNS AND SONGS

Come and Praise
- 2 Have you heard the raindrops drumming on the rooftops?
- 6 The earth is yours, O God

Hymns Ancient and Modern New Standard
- 458 Forth in the peace of Christ we go
- 513 The prophets spoke in days of old

53
SPRING CLEANING

PREPARATION

GOSPEL THEME

The old temple is replaced by the new
(John 2.13–22)

The story of Jesus cleansing the temple occurs in all four gospels. The story is treated very differently by John. While the other three gospels place the story after the Palm Sunday entry to Jerusalem at the beginning of Holy Week, John places the story at the beginning of Jesus' ministry. The key image for John is that Jesus not only cleanses the temple but replaces it. Just as the temple was the meeting place between God and the people of God in the old order, so, after the resurrection, Jesus is that meeting place in the new order. Here is one of the images of Messiahship held out during Lent.

We can begin to experience the significance of the cleansing of the temple by exploring our own images of spring cleaning.

AIMS

- to build on our experiences of spring cleaning;
- to help us understand John's message of cleansing the temple;
- to turn to Jesus as the new temple.

EXPLORING WITH CHILDREN

STARTING

Bring in some cleaning equipment. Discuss spring cleaning, drawing out ideas of:

- general cleaning that is done every day and week;
- what the children do to help;
- special cleaning that is done when the weather warms up;
- what the children do to help;
- how different the house looks when it is clean.

TALKING POINTS

Tell the story from John of Jesus in the temple. As you work, talk with the children about the significance of this. You could include the following points:

- the temple was a place for prayer;
- there was too much noise and activity for prayer;
- Jesus cleaned the people out of the temple;
- Jesus described himself as a temple of God;
- this is a picture of Jesus as Messiah.

ACTIVITIES

- Work together to clean up the room where you meet. Afterwards, enjoy the change you have made.
- Make your own brooms (from twigs) and dusters (from scrap material).
- List all the things in your bedrooms that need spring cleaning. Choose at least one to clean this week.
- With toy farm animals, figures and building blocks, make a model of Jesus cleaning out the temple.

DISPLAY

- Today's theme is the old temple replaced by the new.
- Jesus drove the sellers from the temple.
- Jesus called himself the temple of God.
- Jesus cleaned out the temple.
- Our work today is about spring cleaning.

EXPLORING WITH ADULTS

EXPERIENCE

- What is your experience of spring cleaning?
- What does spring cleaning really achieve?
- Is spring cleaning a helpful image of Jesus' Messiahship?

GOSPEL

- What does this gospel say about the temple?
- How do you interpret this message for today?
- What do you understand by 'the temple of his body'?

APPLICATION

- How helpful is the image of Jesus as the new temple for the church today?
- How helpful is the image of Jesus as the new temple in your devotion today?
- How can the cleansing of the temple be presented in liturgy?

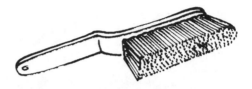

CELEBRATING TOGETHER

WELCOMING CHILDREN

At an appropriate point in the service, invite the children to present their work on spring cleaning. If they have made brooms and dusters, invite them to undertake a symbolic spring cleaning of the church while an appropriate song is sung.

HYMNS AND SONGS

Come and Praise
   5 Carpenter, carpenter, make me a tree
 14 All the nations of the earth

Hymns Ancient and Modern New Standard
 174 O thou not made with hands
 336 All my hope on God is founded

54
GARDENING

PREPARATION

GOSPEL THEME

The fig tree is given a new chance (Luke 13.1–9)

God looks for proper fruit from the people of God, just as the owner of a fig tree looks for fruit from that tree. The gardener gives the fig tree one more chance by nurturing it. So Jesus gives the people of God one more chance. Here is one of the images of Messiahship held out during Lent.

We can begin to experience the significance of Luke's message about the fig tree by exploring our own images of gardening during the spring.

AIMS

● to build on our experiences of springtime gardening;

● to understand Luke's image of tending the fig tree;

● to turn to Jesus to accept the new chance he offers.

EXPLORING WITH CHILDREN

STARTING

Bring in some gardening tools. Discuss gardening, drawing out ideas of:

● gardens the children have at home;

● gardening in window boxes;

● work they have seen being done in a garden;

● other work that gardens require;

● what is happening in gardens now that spring has arrived.

TALKING POINTS

Tell the story from Luke of the fig tree. As you work, talk with the children about the significance of this. You could include the following points:

● fig trees were grown for their fruit;

● this fig tree seemed useless;

● the gardener asked for one more chance;

● Jesus is like the gardener;

● Jesus gives the people of God another chance.

ACTIVITIES

- Prepare a mime about gardening, using a variety of tools.
- Make your own gardens in pots. Plant seedlings. Discuss how to care for them.
- Make a large display of a fig tree. Write thank-you prayers on pieces of paper cut into the shape of figs.
- Work together on the church garden, digging around the plants and putting down compost. (First arrange permission with the site management team.)

DISPLAY

- Today's theme is the fig tree given a new chance.
- The gardener gave the fig tree a new chance.
- A garden is a place of new chances.
- Jesus offers new chances.
- Our work today is about gardening.

EXPLORING WITH ADULTS

EXPERIENCE

- What is your experience of springtime gardening?
- What does springtime gardening achieve?
- Is springtime gardening a helpful image of Jesus' Messiahship?

GOSPEL

- What does this gospel say about the fig tree?
- How do you interpret this message for today?
- What do you understand by 'the gardener'?

APPLICATION

- How helpful is the image of the fig tree for the church today?
- How helpful is the image of the fig tree for your devotions today?
- How can the message of the fig tree be presented in liturgy?

CELEBRATING TOGETHER

WELCOMING CHILDREN

At an appropriate point in the service, invite the children to present their work on springtime gardening. If they have brought garden tools, invite them to present a mime on gardening while an appropriate song is sung.

HYMNS AND SONGS

Come and Praise
   4 Autumn days when the grass is jewelled
 11 For the beauty of the earth

Hymns Ancient and Modern New Standard
342 Awake, awake: fling off the night!
476 Jesus, my Lord

55 MARY CARING FOR JESUS

PREPARATION

GOSPEL THEME

Mary in the temple (Luke 2.33–35)

Traditionally the fourth Sunday of Lent has been kept as Refreshment Sunday or Mothering Sunday. The gospel passage chosen from Luke portrays Mary caring for the infant Jesus as she brings Jesus to the temple together with Joseph. They come to the temple to fulfil a requirement of the Jewish law. There in the temple Mary hears the prophecy of Simeon.

We can begin to experience the significance of Mothering Sunday by focusing attention on the care shown by Mary for her son Jesus.

AIMS

- to develop our image of Mary caring for Jesus;
- to help us understand the responsibility of mothers to their children;
- to give thanks for our own mothers.

EXPLORING WITH CHILDREN

STARTING

Bring in a picture of Mary with the infant Jesus. (Be sensitive in your approach, as some children in your group may not live with a mother.) Discuss this, drawing out ideas of:

- how Mary must have looked after Jesus;
- how women today look after babies;
- the differences between then and now;
- games Mary might have played with Jesus;
- how Mary would have protected Jesus.

TALKING POINTS

Tell the account from Luke of Mary presenting Jesus in the temple. As you work, talk with the children about the significance of this. You could include the following points:

- in Jewish law, babies were taken to the temple;
- they were presented to God;
- Mary and Joseph took Jesus;
- this was one way of caring for him.

ACTIVITIES

- Paint your own pictures of Mary holding Jesus or playing with her baby.
- Invite a mother and young baby to talk about things she needs to do to look after her baby. Prepare a series of black and white pictures with captions to make into a book.
- Prepare a drama about Mary bringing the infant Jesus to the temple and meeting with Simeon.
- Make thank-you cards for your mothers. (Only choose this option if all the children live with their mothers.)

DISPLAY

- Today's theme is Mary in the temple
- Mary presented Jesus in the temple.
- Mothers are responsible for caring for children.
- Mary cared for Jesus.
- Our work today is about Mary caring for Jesus.

EXPLORING WITH ADULTS

EXPERIENCE

- What traditions do you recall of Mary caring for Jesus?
- What pictures do you have in mind of Mary caring for Jesus?
- How helpful is the image of Mary for Mothering Sunday?

GOSPEL

- What does this gospel say about Mary's relationship with Jesus?

- How do you interpret this message for today?
- What do you understand by 'a sword will pierce your own soul too'?

APPLICATION

- What place should Mary have in the life of the church today?
- What place should Mary have in your life today?
- What place should Mary have in liturgy today?

CELEBRATING TOGETHER

WELCOMING CHILDREN

At an appropriate point in the service, invite the children to present their work on Mary caring for Jesus. If the children have prepared a drama about Mary bringing the infant Jesus to the temple and meeting with Simeon, this can be presented after the gospel reading.

HYMNS AND SONGS

Come and Praise
  78 By brother sun who brings the day
102 You can't stop rain

Hymns Ancient and Modern New Standard
104 For the beauty of the earth
360 For Mary, Mother of our Lord

56
JESUS CARING FOR MARY

GOSPEL THEME

Mary at the cross (John 19.25–27)

Traditionally the fourth Sunday of Lent has been kept as Refreshment Sunday or Mothering Sunday. The gospel passage chosen from John portrays Mary standing by the cross of Jesus. At this time of agony Jesus displays care and concern for his mother.

We can begin to experience the significance of Mothering Sunday by focusing attention on the care shown by Jesus for his mother Mary.

AIMS

● to develop our image of Jesus caring for Mary;

● to help us understand the responsibility of children to their mothers;

● to consider our responsibility to our own mothers.

STARTING

Bring in a picture of a child helping its mother. (If you have a child in your group who does not live with his or her mother, extend the discussion to stepmothers and other carers.) Discuss it, drawing out ideas of:

● what is happening in the picture;

● times the children have helped their mothers;

● things they do to help;

● why we help our parents;

● how we feel when we choose to help.

TALKING POINTS

Tell the story from John of Jesus caring for Mary. As you work, talk with the children about the significance of this. You could include the following points:

● Mary had cared for Jesus when he was young;

● when Jesus was older he looked after his mother;

● now he was dying he would not be able to help her;

● he arranged for John to look after her instead;

● Jesus loved his mother.

ACTIVITIES

- Make a display of pictures and statues of Mary, including some the children paint or draw themselves.
- Make a list of ways that you can help your own mothers. Make a card promising to do one of these this week.
- Make up a drama or dance about children helping their mother.
- Interview 'Mary' and 'John' about their feelings at Jesus' words.

DISPLAY

- Today's theme is Mary at the cross.
- Jesus looked after his mother.
- We can help our mothers.
- Mary needed Jesus.
- Our work today is about Jesus caring for Mary.

EXPLORING WITH ADULTS

EXPERIENCE

- What traditions do you recall of Jesus caring for Mary?
- What pictures do you have in mind of Jesus caring for Mary?
- How helpful is the image of Mary for Mothering Sunday?

GOSPEL

- What does this gospel say about Jesus' relationship with Mary?
- How do you interpret this message for today?
- What do you understand by 'Woman, behold your son'?

APPLICATION

- What place should Mary have in the life of the church today?
- What place should Mary have in your life today?
- What place should Mary have in liturgy today?

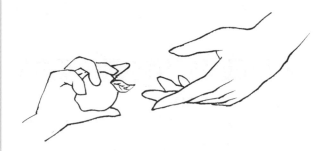

CELEBRATING TOGETHER

WELCOMING CHILDREN

At an appropriate point in the service, invite the children to present their work on Jesus caring for Mary. If the children have collected pictures of Mary, these can be displayed during the gospel reading.

HYMNS AND SONGS

Come and Praise
  9 Fill your hearts with joy and gladness
25 When Jesus walked in Galilee

Hymns Ancient and Modern New Standard
482 Life is great! So sing about it
494 Lord of the home, your only Son

57
MARY TODAY

PREPARATION

GOSPEL THEME

Mary in the temple (Luke 2.33–35)

Traditionally the fourth Sunday of Lent has been kept as Refreshment Sunday or Mothering Sunday. The gospel passage chosen from Luke highlights Mary's close identification with the ministry and suffering of her son Jesus. The significance given to Mary within the Christian tradition differs considerably from one church to another. Mothering Sunday provides an appropriate occasion to reflect on the place of Mary in different churches today.

We can begin to experience the significance of Mothering Sunday by focusing attention on the place accorded to Mary in different churches.

AIMS

● to build on our images of Mary in the church;

● to help us understand the significance of Mary to different Christians;

● to value the place of women in the church.

EXPLORING WITH CHILDREN

STARTING

Bring in a picture of Mary. Discuss it, drawing out ideas of:

● pictures of Mary the children may have at home;

● other pictures of Mary they may have seen;

● places where they have seen such pictures;

● what the pictures tell us about Mary;

● what the pictures tell us of the way people feel about Mary.

TALKING POINTS

Tell the story from Luke of Simeon's words to Mary. As you work, talk with the children about the significance of this. You could include the following points:

● we know how much Jesus suffered on the cross;

● Mary suffered too, to see him there;

● Mary was told shortly after his birth that she would suffer;

● all Jesus' life, Mary must have known about this pain to come;

● we can admire, respect and love Mary.

ACTIVITIES

- Find out about the places of pilgrimage inspired by Mary, such as Walsingham, Knock or Lourdes. Look at these places in an atlas and find out how far from you they are. Make a display of pictures.
- Look through a selection of books to find pictures of Mary and to see what is said about her.
- Look around your own church for pictures and statues of Mary.
- Paint pictures of Mary or make clay statues.

DISPLAY

- Today's theme is Mary in the temple.
- Mary knew she would suffer too.
- We respect and love Mary.
- We think about Mary's work and her suffering.
- Our work is about attitudes to Mary today.

EXPLORING WITH ADULTS

EXPERIENCE

- What are your experiences of churches and places devoted to Mary?
- What is your view of Mary today?
- How helpful is the image of Mary for Mothering Sunday?

GOSPEL

- What does this gospel say about Mary?
- How do you interpret this message for today?
- What do you understand from the attention which Luke gives to Mary?

APPLICATION

- What place should Mary have in the life of the church today?
- What place should Mary have in your life today?
- What place should Mary have in liturgy today?

CELEBRATING TOGETHER

WELCOMING CHILDREN

At an appropriate point in the service, invite the children to present their work on Mary today. If pictures have been obtained of one of the places of pilgrimage inspired by Mary (such as Walsingham, Knock or Lourdes), these can be displayed during the gospel reading.

HYMNS AND SONGS

Come and Praise
   85 Spirit of peace, come to our waiting world
   87 Give us hope, Lord, for each day

Hymns Ancient and Modern New Standard
  104 For the beauty of the earth
  394 Lord of all hopefulness, Lord of all joy

58
TOMBS

PREPARATION

GOSPEL THEME

The raising of Lazarus (John 11.1–45)

The fifth Sunday of Lent prepares the people of God for the events of Holy Week when Jesus will be arrested and crucified. They approach the death of Jesus in confidence of the resurrection. In John's gospel the raising of Lazarus prefigures Jesus' own resurrection and provides the context for Jesus' teaching 'I am the resurrection and the life'.

We can begin to experience the significance of John's message about Jesus as the resurrection and the life by exploring the tombs and gravestones around our own church, together with their messages of promise in life beyond the grave.

AIMS

● to build on our experiences of tombs and the promise of life;

● to help us understand the raising of Lazarus as the promise of life;

● to prepare us for the crucifixion and death of Jesus.

EXPLORING WITH CHILDREN

STARTING

Take the children out to the graveyard or bring in a picture of a tombstone. Discuss this, drawing out ideas of:

● times the children have been in graveyards;

● any gravestones they have especially noticed;

● the variety of gravestones;

● messages of hope that are engraved on tombs;

● these remind us of the Christian promise of life.

TALKING POINTS

Tell the story from John of the raising of Lazarus. As you work, talk with the children about the significance of this. You could include the following points:

● Jesus arrived four days after Lazarus was put in the tomb;

● Jesus said 'I am the resurrection and the life';

● Jesus brought Lazarus back to life;

● Christians have been given the promise of life;

● we remember this during Lent when we prepare for Jesus' death.

ACTIVITIES

- Visit the graveyard and look for inscriptions presenting the Christian hope. Write these down.
- Design a tomb or gravestone with your own message of hope on it.
- Write a special edition of the 'Bethany Times' about Jesus and Lazarus. Include 'photographs' and advertisements.
- Prepare a dance of the weeping relatives and friends whose grief turns to joy when Lazarus is brought back to life.

DISPLAY

- Today's theme is the raising of Lazarus.
- Jesus said 'I am the resurrection and the life'.
- Jesus promises us life.
- In Lent we prepare for Jesus' death and resurrection.
- Our work today is about tombs.

EXPLORING WITH ADULTS

EXPERIENCE

- What are your experiences of tombs?
- What messages have you seen on tombs?
- Do tombs move you to sadness or to hope?

GOSPEL

- What does this gospel say about death?
- How do you interpret this message for today?
- What do you understand by 'I am the resurrection and the life'?

APPLICATION

- How should the church proclaim the raising of Lazarus today?
- What part should this story play in your preparation for Holy Week?
- How should the resurrection be presented in liturgy?

CELEBRATING TOGETHER

WELCOMING CHILDREN

At an appropriate point in the service, invite the children to present their work on tombs. If the children have collated inscriptions from tombs presenting the Christian hope, these can be read aloud after the gospel reading.

HYMNS AND SONGS

Come and Praise
26 There is singing in the desert
54 The King of love my shepherd is

Hymns Ancient and Modern New Standard
65 My God, I love thee; not because
496 Morning glory, starlit sky

59
SEEDS

GOSPEL THEME

The grain of wheat (John 12.20–33)

The fifth Sunday of Lent prepares the people of God for the events of Holy Week when Jesus will be arrested and crucified. They approach the death of Jesus in confidence of the resurrection. In John's gospel Jesus offers the model of the grain of wheat being buried in the earth and dying before growing into new life. This model prefigures Jesus' own death.

We can begin to experience the significance of Jesus' teaching on the grain of wheat by exploring our own experiences of seeds dying and germinating.

AIMS

- to build on our experiences of seeds dying and germinating;
- to help us understand the grain of wheat as the promise of life;
- to prepare us for the crucifixion and death of Jesus.

EXPLORING WITH CHILDREN

STARTING

Bring in some seeds. Look at these and feel and discuss them, drawing out ideas of:

- the dry, shrivelled appearance of the seeds;
- their tiny size;
- other seeds the children have seen;
- seeds the children have planted;
- what grew from them.

TALKING POINTS

Tell of Jesus' words from John. As you work, talk with the children about the significance of these. You could include the following points:

- Jesus knew that he would soon die and be resurrected;
- he reminded his followers of wheat seeds;
- the seeds look dead;
- when they are buried and 'die', they produce plants;
- this picture gives us confidence of life with Jesus.

ACTIVITIES

- Prepare a dance of seeds being buried in the soil, dying and sprouting to new life.
- Cut cross shapes from cotton wool and put them on foil plates. Cover them with fast-growing seeds such as cress. Encourage each child to take one home and water it, keeping it in a dark cupboard for the first few days.
- Prepare cards of hope to give people, showing a seed or bulb on the front and a pop-up flower inside.
- Arrange for some children to grow mustard and cress in the preceding week so that all can see the growth.

DISPLAY

- Today's theme is the grain of wheat.
- Jesus said that seeds must die to produce fruit.
- Jesus promises us life.
- In Lent we prepare for Jesus' death and resurrection.
- Our work today is about seeds.

EXPLORING WITH ADULTS

EXPERIENCE

- What are your experiences of seeds dying and growing?
- Does the seed really bring you promise of life?
- How helpful is the image of the seed to prepare for Holy Week?

GOSPEL

- What does this gospel say about the death of Jesus?

- How do you interpret this message for today?
- What do you understand by Jesus' reference to 'much fruit'?

APPLICATION

- How should the church proclaim the message of the grain of wheat today?
- What part should this story play in your preparation for Holy Week?
- How should the grain of wheat be presented in liturgy?

CELEBRATING TOGETHER

WELCOMING CHILDREN

At an appropriate point in the service, invite the children to present their work on seeds. If the children have prepared a dance illustrating the seed being buried in the soil, dying, and sprouting to new life, this can be presented after the gospel reading.

HYMNS AND SONGS

Come and Praise
29 From the darkness came light
131 Now the green blade rises

Hymns Ancient and Modern New Standard
63 My song is love unknown
487 Lord Christ, we praise your sacrifice

60 FUNERALS

PREPARATION

GOSPEL THEME

Anointing Jesus' feet (John 12.1–8)

The fifth Sunday of Lent prepares the people of God for the events of Holy Week when Jesus will be arrested and crucified. They approach the death of Jesus in confidence of the resurrection. In John's gospel, when Mary anointed Jesus' feet with costly perfume she prefigured his burial. But all this was done in the very place where Lazarus had already been raised from the dead. So, too, will Jesus be raised from the dead after his burial.

We can begin to experience the significance of John's message about the burial of Jesus by exploring our own ideas of funerals.

AIMS

- to build on our own experiences of funerals;
- to help us understand Jesus' burial as the preparation for resurrection;
- to prepare us for the crucifixion and death of Jesus.

EXPLORING WITH CHILDREN

STARTING

Bring in a bottle of perfume or ointment. Discuss this, drawing out ideas of:

- whether or not the children like the smell;
- people they know who use perfume and ointment;
- times that perfume or ointment are used;
- times they have used it themselves;
- in olden days, perfumed ointments were used for funerals.

TALKING POINTS

Tell the story from John of Mary anointing Jesus' feet. As you work, talk with the children about the significance of this. You could include the following points:

- Mary poured expensive perfume over Jesus' feet;
- Judas thought it should have been sold to help the poor;
- Jesus said Mary had done a good thing;
- this perfume was to serve for his burial;
- we remember that Jesus' resurrection followed his burial.

ACTIVITIES

- Prepare a drama about Mary anointing Jesus' feet.
- Learn the Sydney Carter song 'Judas and Mary' and prepare a mime to go with it.
- Make flower wreaths from real or paper flowers. Place these in an appropriate spot in memory of Jesus' death.
- Write funeral notices for Jesus' death, including information about Mary anointing Jesus.

DISPLAY

- Today's theme is Mary anointing Jesus' feet.
- Mary prepared for Jesus' burial.
- We thought about funerals.
- In Lent we prepare for Jesus' death and resurrection.
- Our work today is about funerals.

EXPLORING WITH ADULTS

EXPERIENCE

- What are your experiences of funerals?
- Have you experienced funerals as a sign of hope?
- What makes a good funeral?

GOSPEL

- What does this gospel say about the death of Jesus?
- How do you interpret this message for today?
- What do you understand by Mary's action?

APPLICATION

- How should the church proclaim this story today?
- What part should this story play in your preparation for Holy Week?
- How should the anointing of Jesus' feet be presented in liturgy?

CELEBRATING TOGETHER

WELCOMING CHILDREN

At an appropriate point in the service, invite the children to present their work on funerals. If the children have prepared a drama on Mary anointing Jesus' feet, this can be presented after the gospel reading.

HYMNS AND SONGS

Come and Praise
  25 When Jesus walked in Galilee
  28 Said Judas to Mary

Hymns Ancient and Modern New Standard
  66 Glory be to Jesus
 497 Nature with open volume stands

61
PROCESSIONAL CROSSES

PREPARATION

GOSPEL THEME

Jesus' entry into Jerusalem (Matthew 21.1–11)

The events of Holy Week begin with Jesus' triumphal entry into Jerusalem. Each of the three synoptic gospels tells the story in a slightly different way, but the key idea remains the same. Drawing on imagery from the Old Testament, the gospel writers make it plain that Jesus is entering Jerusalem as Messiah. Many local churches now capture the Palm Sunday theme by arranging a procession through the streets. Some of these processions even include a donkey.

We can begin to experience the significance of Matthew's account of the Palm Sunday journey by making our own processional crosses to share in a re-enactment of the entry into Jerusalem.

AIMS

- to build on our images of processional crosses;
- to enter the spirit of the Palm Sunday journey to Jerusalem;
- to walk alongside Jesus through Holy Week.

EXPLORING WITH CHILDREN

STARTING

Bring in some balloons to blow up and hand out. Discuss them, drawing out ideas of:

- times the children have used balloons;
- other times that balloons are displayed;
- the way we feel when we see balloons;
- the use of balloons in processions and celebrations;
- the church uses the cross in procession.

TALKING POINTS

Tell the story from Matthew of Jesus' entry into Jerusalem. As you work, talk with the children about the significance of this. You could include the following points:

- Jesus was on the way to Jerusalem;
- the crowd spread cloaks on the road for him;
- some spread palm branches on the road;
- they celebrated and praised the coming of Jesus;
- the church today still celebrates Jesus' coming.

ACTIVITIES

- Make large processional crosses from cardboard or wood.
- Make badges in the shape of palm leaves or crosses.
- Help to make palm crosses for use in the service.
- Prepare a re-enactment of the first Palm Sunday.

DISPLAY

- Today's theme is Jesus' entry into Jerusalem.
- We celebrate Palm Sunday.
- The crowds welcomed Jesus to Jerusalem.
- The church welcomes Jesus today.
- Our work today is about processional crosses.

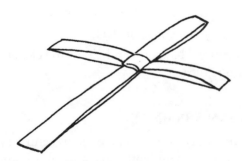

EXPLORING WITH ADULTS

EXPERIENCE

- What are your experiences of processional crosses?
- Where have you seen processional crosses?
- How appropriate are processional crosses to Palm Sunday?

GOSPEL

- What does this gospel say about Jesus' entry into Jerusalem?
- How do you interpret this message for today?
- What do you understand by people cutting branches from the trees?

APPLICATION

- How should the church make best use of processional crosses?
- How should processional crosses focus your devotions?
- How can the church best present the theme of Palm Sunday?

CELEBRATING TOGETHER

WELCOMING CHILDREN

If the church arranges a Palm Sunday procession, make sure that good use is made of the processional crosses produced by the children. If the church does not arrange a procession, these crosses can be held high during the gospel reading.

HYMNS AND SONGS

Come and Praise
45 The journey of life
128 Trotting, trotting through Jerusalem

Hymns Ancient and Modern New Standard
61 Ride on, ride on in majesty!
117 Praise to the Holiest in the height

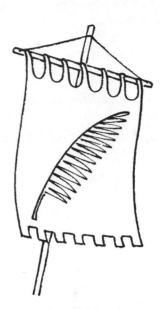

62 PROCESSIONAL BANNERS

PREPARATION

GOSPEL THEME

Jesus' entry into Jerusalem (Mark 11.1–11)

The events of Holy Week begin with Jesus' triumphal entry into Jerusalem. Each of the three synoptic gospels tells the story in a slightly different way, but the key idea remains the same. Drawing on imagery from the Old Testament, the gospel writers make it plain that Jesus is entering Jerusalem as Messiah. Many local churches now capture the Palm Sunday theme by arranging a procession through the streets. Some of these processions even include a donkey.

We can begin to experience the significance of Mark's account of the Palm Sunday journey by making our own processional banners to share in a re-enactment of the entry into Jerusalem.

AIMS

- to build on our images of processional banners;
- to enter the spirit of the Palm Sunday journey to Jerusalem;
- to walk alongside Jesus through Holy Week.

EXPLORING WITH CHILDREN

STARTING

Bring in some streamers or party poppers. Discuss these, drawing out ideas of:

- the children's reactions to them;
- events where streamers and party poppers are used;
- times the children have used these;
- the way they make us feel;
- in church, banners can help us to celebrate and rejoice.

TALKING POINTS

Tell the story from Mark of Jesus' entry into Jerusalem. As you work, talk with the children about the significance of this. You could include the following points:

- Jesus was on the way to Jerusalem;
- the crowd spread cloaks on the road for him;
- some spread palm branches on the road;
- they celebrated and praised the coming of Jesus;
- the church today still celebrates Jesus' coming.

ACTIVITIES

- Make banners to use in a Palm Sunday procession or in church. For use outside, these could be old sheets with designs glued or painted on them.
- Make smaller banners to display at home.
- Compose music for the first Palm Sunday, including a steady beat for the colt, swooshing noises for the cloaks and branches, and triumphal cheers.
- Make a wall mural of palm leaves with words such as 'We welcome Jesus'.

DISPLAY

- Today's theme is Jesus' entry into Jerusalem.
- We celebrate Palm Sunday.
- The crowds welcomed Jesus to Jerusalem.
- The church welcomes Jesus today.
- Our work today is about processional banners.

EXPLORING WITH ADULTS

EXPERIENCE

- What are your experiences of processional banners?
- Where have you seen processional banners?
- How appropriate are processional banners for Palm Sunday?

GOSPEL

- What does this gospel say about Jesus' entry into Jerusalem?
- How do you interpret this message for today?
- What do you understand by Jesus riding a colt?

APPLICATION

- How should the church make best use of processional banners?
- How should processional banners focus your devotion?
- How can the church best present the theme of Palm Sunday?

CELEBRATING TOGETHER

WELCOMING CHILDREN

If the church arranges a Palm Sunday procession, make sure that good use is made of the processional banners produced by the children. If the church does not arrange a procession, these banners can be held high during the gospel reading.

HYMNS AND SONGS

Come and Praise
 34 Praise to the Lord
128 Trotting, trotting through Jerusalem

Hymns Ancient and Modern New Standard
 60 All glory, laud, and honour
148 At the name of Jesus

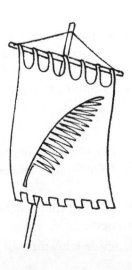

63
PROCESSIONAL ROBES

PREPARATION

GOSPEL THEME

Jesus' entry into Jerusalem (Luke 19.28–40)

The events of Holy Week begin with Jesus' triumphal entry into Jerusalem. Each of the three synoptic gospels tells the story in a slightly different way, but the key idea remains the same. Drawing on imagery from the Old Testament, the gospel writers make it plain that Jesus is entering Jerusalem as Messiah. Many local churches now capture the Palm Sunday theme by arranging a procession through the streets. Some of these processions even include a donkey.

We can begin to experience the significance of Luke's account of the Palm Sunday journey by making our own processional robes to identify with those original Palestine people who formed the first Palm Sunday procession.

AIMS

- to build on our images of how people in the original Palm Sunday procession were dressed;
- to enter the spirit of the Palm Sunday journey to Jerusalem;
- to walk alongside Jesus through Holy Week.

EXPLORING WITH CHILDREN

STARTING

Bring in some party hats. Discuss these, drawing out ideas of:

- the children's reactions to them;
- events where party hats are used;
- times the children have worn party hats;
- the way they make us feel;
- in church, processional robes help us to celebrate and rejoice.

TALKING POINTS

Tell the story from Luke of Jesus' entry into Jerusalem. As you work, talk with the children about the significance of this. You could include the following points:

- Jesus was on the way to Jerusalem;
- the crowd spread cloaks on the road for him;
- they celebrated the coming of Jesus;
- they praised God for all that Jesus had done;
- the church today still celebrates Jesus' coming.

ACTIVITIES

- Use old sheets and curtains to make robes such as those worn by Jesus' followers.
- Dress dolls or cardboard figures in clothes like the early disciples.
- Devise a dance of swirling cloaks (use towels or pieces of cloth), ending with these on the 'road'.
- Design cards for Palm Sunday with a design of cloaks and a special message of celebration

DISPLAY

- Today's theme is Jesus' entry into Jerusalem.
- We celebrate Palm Sunday.
- The crowds welcomed Jesus to Jerusalem.
- The church welcomes Jesus today.
- Our work today is about processional robes.

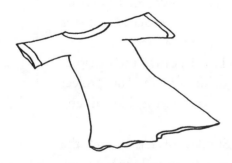

EXPLORING WITH ADULTS

EXPERIENCE

- Who do you imagine were present on the first Palm Sunday?
- How do you imagine these people were dressed?
- How helpful do you find it to get inside the costume of a past age?

GOSPEL

- What does this gospel say about Jesus' entry into Jerusalem?
- How do you interpret this message for today?
- What do you understand by people spreading their cloaks on the road?

APPLICATION

- How should the church make best use of the Palm Sunday procession?
- How should you make best use of the Palm Sunday procession?
- How can the church encourage more people to share in the Palm Sunday procession?

CELEBRATING TOGETHER

WELCOMING CHILDREN

If the church arranges a Palm Sunday procession, make sure that good use is made of the processional robes produced by the children. If the church does not arrange a procession, these robes can be worn and displayed during the gospel reading.

HYMNS AND SONGS

Come and Praise
   7 All creatures of our God and King
128 Trotting, trotting through Jerusalem

Hymns Ancient and Modern New Standard
  62 Ride on triumphantly! Behold, we lay
337 All praise to thee, for thou, O King divine

Introduction to the Season of Easter

The season of Easter begins with Easter Sunday and concludes with the Day of Pentecost. There are six Sundays between these two major festivals.

The gospel readings for Easter Sunday tell the story of the empty tomb from the perspectives of the three synoptic gospels. The project activities set alongside the fact of the empty tomb powerful images of the new life to which the empty tomb points. The three images selected are Easter eggs, spring flowers and the tortoise who wakens from hibernation.

The gospel reading for the second Sunday of Easter presents John's account of Jesus appearing to the disciples on the evening of Easter Day and then again a week later on Easter octave. While on Easter Sunday the emphasis is on the empty tomb, on the second Sunday of Easter the emphasis is on the evidence for the resurrection. The project activities focus on the grounds for this evidence: seeing, touching and hearing.

The gospel readings for the third Sunday of Easter portray the disciples meeting with the risen Jesus in the ordinary affairs of life. The project activities capture this theme by focusing on ordinary events, like sharing bread, eating fish and having breakfast.

The gospel readings between the fourth Sunday of Easter and the seventh Sunday of Easter all focus on images of Jesus from John's gospel. This cycle begins on the fourth Sunday of Easter with three images of Jesus the good shepherd. The project activities develop this theme by exploring sheep, shepherds and sheepdogs.

The fifth Sunday of Easter follows the theme of the good shepherd with the three images of the way, the vine, and the new commandment. The project activities develop these themes by exploring maps, vines and hearts.

The sixth Sunday of Easter draws to a close the period of the resurrection appearances and anticipates the Ascension and the Day of Pentecost. The gospel readings are from the farewell discourses of John and point to the ongoing life of the Christian community after Jesus is taken from them and the Holy Spirit has been sent to them. The project activities develop this theme by exploring ideas of the team, the coach and the guide.

The seventh Sunday of Easter is also the Sunday following the ascension. The project activities explore the ascension in terms of the kingship of Christ by looking at royal crowns, royal robes and royal thrones.

The season of Easter comes to a close with the Day of Pentecost when the early church received the gift of the Holy Spirit. The project activities explore three of the major images associated with the Holy Spirit in wind, fire and birds.

64
EASTER EGGS

GOSPEL THEME

The empty tomb (Matthew 28.1–10)

Matthew tells the story of the first Easter morning with considerable theatrical effect. There was an earthquake, the angel's appearance was like lightning and the guards shook with fear. At the heart of the narrative, however, stands the stark and simple message of the empty tomb. The angelic messenger spells out the implications: 'He is not here; for he has been raised, as he said. Come, see the place where he lay.' The empty tomb points to the Easter message of new life.

We can begin to pass beyond the empty tomb to experience the gospel message of new life by exploring classic images of new life, like the Easter egg.

AIMS

- to build on our experiences of Easter eggs;
- to help us see Easter eggs as a symbol of new life;
- to celebrate the new life of the empty tomb.

STARTING

Give a small Easter egg to each child to eat. Discuss these, drawing out ideas of:

- their feelings at seeing and eating Easter eggs;
- eggs the children have received this Easter;
- eggs the children have given this Easter;
- real eggs the children have seen, such as in nests;
- eggs are an image of new life.

TALKING POINTS

Tell the story from Matthew of the empty tomb. As you work, talk with the children about the significance of this. You could include the following points:

- Jesus was buried on Friday night, just before the Sabbath;
- early on the Sunday morning the women went to the tomb;
- Jesus' body was not there; he had been raised;
- Jesus met the women and they touched him;
- Jesus said he would meet the disciples in Galilee.

ACTIVITIES

- If you have small plastic Easter egg moulds, make chocolate eggs.
- Decorate hard-boiled eggs or blown eggs to give away.
- Decorate badges in the shape of Easter eggs to give to those in the congregation.
- Make Easter cards celebrating Jesus' new life.

DISPLAY

- Today's theme is the empty tomb.
- Jesus was raised to new life at Easter.
- We celebrate new life at Easter.
- Eggs are a symbol of new life.
- Our work today is about Easter eggs.

EXPLORING WITH ADULTS

EXPERIENCE

- What are your experiences of Easter eggs?
- With what ideas and images are Easter eggs associated in your mind?
- How useful is the Easter egg as a symbol of new life?

GOSPEL

- What does this gospel say about the empty tomb?
- How do you interpret this message for today?
- What do you understand by the angel's insistence 'to see the place'?

APPLICATION

- How should the church present the message of the empty tomb today?
- How should you understand the message of the empty tomb today?
- How should the empty tomb be proclaimed in liturgy?

CELEBRATING TOGETHER

WELCOMING CHILDREN

At an appropriate point in the service, invite the children to present their work on Easter eggs. If the children have made sufficient Easter-egg-shaped badges, these can be shared with the congregation as a symbol of new life.

HYMNS AND SONGS

Come and Praise
   25 When Jesus walked in Galilee
  131 Now the green blade rises

Hymns Ancient and Modern New Standard
   78 The strife is o'er, the battle done
   84 The Lord is risen indeed

65
SPRING FLOWERS

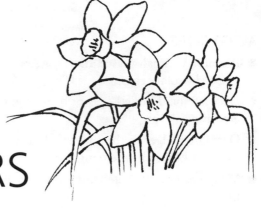

PREPARATION

GOSPEL THEME

The empty tomb (Mark 16.1–8)

Mark tells the story of the first Easter morning with stark simplicity. The women simply see that the stone has been rolled away and they meet a young man dressed in a white robe. They leave in fear. At the heart of the narrative stands the message of the empty tomb. The angelic messenger spells out the implications: 'He has been raised; he is not here. Look, there is the place they laid him.' The empty tomb points to the Easter message of new life.

We can begin to pass beyond the empty tomb to experience the gospel message of new life by exploring classic images of new life, like spring flowers.

AIMS

- to build on our experiences of spring flowers;
- to help us see spring flowers as a symbol of new life;
- to celebrate the new life of the empty tomb.

EXPLORING WITH CHILDREN

STARTING

Bring in a bulb and a pot of spring flowers. Discuss these, drawing out ideas of:

- spring flowers the children have growing at home;
- spring flowers the children have seen in local parks;
- the way the bulb itself looks dead;
- the beauty and life of the flowers that have grown from the bulb;
- spring flowers are an image of new life.

TALKING POINTS

Tell the story from Mark of the empty tomb. As you work, talk with the children about the significance of this. You could include the following points:

- Jesus was buried on Friday night, just before the Sabbath;
- early on the Sunday morning the women went to the tomb;
- the stone in front of the tomb had been rolled away;
- Jesus' body was not there; he had been raised;
- they were told that Jesus would meet them in Galilee.

ACTIVITIES

- Make a display of spring flowers with a sign about new life. If you do not have enough real flowers, you could make paper flowers to add to the display.
- Make Easter cards celebrating Jesus' new life.
- Plant spring seedlings in individual pots for the children to take home and care for as a reminder of new life.
- Make an Easter garden containing small spring flowers.

DISPLAY

- Today's theme is the empty tomb.
- Jesus was raised to new life at Easter.
- We celebrate new life at Easter.
- Spring flowers are a symbol of new life.
- Our work today is about spring flowers.

EXPLORING WITH ADULTS

EXPERIENCE

- What are your experiences of spring flowers?
- With what ideas and images are spring flowers associated in your mind?
- How useful are spring flowers as a symbol of new life?

GOSPEL

- What does this gospel say about the empty tomb?
- How do you interpret this message for today?
- How do you interpret the command 'Look, there is the place'?

APPLICATION

- How can the church encourage people to hear the message of the empty tomb?
- How can you help others to hear the message of the empty tomb?
- How should the empty tomb be proclaimed in liturgy?

CELEBRATING TOGETHER

WELCOMING CHILDREN

At an appropriate point in the service, invite the children to present their work on spring flowers. If the children have organized displays of spring flowers, these can be included in the offertory procession.

HYMNS AND SONGS

Come and Praise
    1 Morning has broken
130 All in an Easter garden

Hymns Ancient and Modern New Standard
  79 Christ the Lord is risen again
501 Now the green blade riseth from the buried grain

66
TORTOISE

GOSPEL THEME

The empty tomb (Luke 24.1–12)

Luke recounts how the women came to the tomb on the first Easter morning. They found the stone rolled away from the tomb, but when they went in, they did not find the body. Then the two men in dazzling clothes spell out the implications of the empty tomb: 'He is not here, but has risen.' The empty tomb points to the Easter message of new life.

We can begin to pass beyond the empty tomb to experience the gospel message of new life by exploring classic images of new life, like the tortoise coming to new life after winter hibernation.

AIMS

- to build on our experiences of tortoises;
- to help us see the tortoise as a symbol of new life;
- to celebrate the new life of the empty tomb.

STARTING

Bring in a tortoise or a picture of one. Discuss this, drawing out ideas of:

- tortoises the children have seen;
- how one looks after a tortoise;
- the tortoise hibernates in winter;
- the tortoise returns to new life in spring;
- the awakening tortoise is an image of new life.

TALKING POINTS

Tell the story from Luke of the empty tomb. As you work, talk with the children about the significance of this. You could include the following points:

- Jesus was buried on Friday night, just before the Sabbath;
- early on the Sunday morning the women went to the tomb;
- Jesus' body was not there; he had been raised;
- they were told that Jesus would meet them in Galilee;
- Peter looked inside the tomb and saw the empty grave clothes.

ACTIVITIES

- Prepare a dance on the tortoise waking up from hibernation.
- Make Easter cards to celebrate Jesus' new life.
- Interview the women and Peter about their Easter experience.
- Write an acrostic on EASTER, using each letter as the start of a word about new life or about Jesus' resurrection.

DISPLAY

- Today's theme is the empty tomb.
- Jesus was raised to new life at Easter.
- We celebrate new life at Easter.
- The awakening tortoise is a symbol of new life.
- Our work today is about the tortoise.

EXPLORING WITH ADULTS

EXPERIENCE

- What are your experiences of tortoises?
- With what ideas and images are tortoises associated in your mind?
- How useful is the tortoise as a symbol of new life?

GOSPEL

- What does this gospel say about the empty tomb?

- How do you interpret this message for today?
- How do you understand Peter's action?

APPLICATION

- How can the church help people to respond to the empty tomb?
- How can you help people to respond to the empty tomb?
- How should the empty tomb be proclaimed in liturgy?

CELEBRATING TOGETHER

WELCOMING CHILDREN

At an appropriate point in the service, invite the children to present their work on tortoises. If the children have prepared a dance on the tortoise waking up from hibernation, this can be presented after the gospel reading.

HYMNS AND SONGS

Come and Praise
130 All in an Easter garden
132 When from the sky in the splendour of summer

Hymns Ancient and Modern New Standard
77 Jesus Christ is risen today
428 Thine be the glory, risen, conquering son

67 SEEING

PREPARATION

GOSPEL THEME

The risen Jesus (John 20.19–31)

John's gospel portrays Jesus coming and standing among his disciples on the evening of Easter Day. Thomas, who was not present when Jesus came, refused to believe without proper evidence. A week later (the second Sunday of Easter) Jesus came and stood among his disciples again. This time Thomas was there and Jesus provided him with the evidence he needed. Thomas saw and heard and touched the risen Jesus, and then he believed. But Jesus said 'Blessed are those who have not seen and yet have come to believe'.

We can begin to share Thomas's concern for evidence by exploring the importance we attach to seeing things for ourselves.

AIMS

- to build on our experiences of seeing things and people;
- to help us understand Thomas's quest to see for himself;
- to help us believe although we have not seen the risen Jesus.

EXPLORING WITH CHILDREN

STARTING

Ask the children to close their eyes and name as many things in the room as they can. Open eyes and discuss this, drawing out ideas of:

- the number of things they could name;
- the number of things they had forgotten;
- if they doubted others who named things they had not noticed;
- how important our sight is;
- the phrase 'seeing is believing'.

TALKING POINTS

Tell the story from John of the resurrection appearance. As you work, talk with the children about the significance of this. You could include the following points:

- the disciples saw Jesus and believed he was risen;
- Thomas was not there and did not believe;
- a week later Jesus came again;
- Thomas believed as soon as he saw him;
- we have not seen Jesus but we can believe in the evidence of others.

ACTIVITIES

- Assemble a series of pictures (perhaps of different types of cars) and look for the identifying features that help you recognize what make it is. Prepare a quiz on these pictures.

- Choose a place that one of you knows well. Let everyone else make a list of things they would expect to be at that place, then the person who has seen the place can tell what is really there.

- In pairs, draw pictures of each other, focusing on the details you can see.

- Interview 'Thomas' about what made him change his mind, or interview a member of the congregation about why he or she believes in Jesus without having seen him.

DISPLAY

- Today's theme is the risen Jesus.
- Thomas saw Jesus and believed.
- We have not seen Jesus but we believe he lives.
- Jesus appeared to the disciples.
- Our work today is about seeing.

EXPLORING WITH ADULTS

EXPERIENCE

- What are your experiences of 'seeing is believing'?

- When have you believed something without seeing?

- Is it possible to test everything by seeing for yourself?

GOSPEL

- What does this gospel say about seeing Jesus?

- How do you interpret this message for today?

- What do you understand by Thomas seeing the mark of the nails?

APPLICATION

- How should the church respond to the request to see Jesus today?

- What should you say to people who want to see Jesus for themselves?

- How should the church proclaim the physical resurrection of Jesus?

CELEBRATING TOGETHER

WELCOMING CHILDREN

At an appropriate point in the service, invite the children to present their work on seeing. If a series of pictures has been assembled (say of different types of cars), these can be displayed as a quiz during the ministry of the word to demonstrate how we recognize things by seeing them for ourselves.

HYMNS AND SONGS

Come and Praise
   18 He gave me eyes so I could see
   34 Praise to the Lord

Hymns Ancient and Modern New Standard
   74 O sons and daughters, let us sing!
  245 Jesus, these eyes have never seen

68 TOUCHING

PREPARATION

GOSPEL THEME

The risen Jesus (John 20.19–31)

John's gospel portrays Jesus coming and standing among his disciples on the evening of Easter Day. Thomas, who was not present when Jesus came, refused to believe without proper evidence. A week later (the second Sunday of Easter) Jesus came and stood among his disciples again. This time Thomas was there and Jesus provided him with the evidence he needed. Thomas saw and heard and touched the risen Jesus, and then he believed. But Jesus said 'Blessed are those who have not seen and yet have come to believe'.

We can begin to share Thomas's concern for evidence by exploring the importance we attach to touching things for ourselves.

AIMS

- to build on our experiences of touching things and people;
- to help us understand Thomas's quest to touch for himself;
- to help us believe although we have not touched the risen Jesus.

EXPLORING WITH CHILDREN

STARTING

Blindfold one child and ask him or her to identify a second child by touch. Discuss this, drawing out ideas of:

- what helped in the identification;
- times (such as power failures) the children have had to rely on touch;
- things the children can identify by touch;
- how hard or easy it is to work out things by touch;
- the phrase 'touching is believing'.

TALKING POINTS

Tell the story from John of the resurrection appearance. As you work, talk with the children about the significance of this. You could include the following points:

- the disciples saw Jesus and believed he was risen;
- Thomas was not there and did not believe;
- he wanted to touch Jesus before he would believe;
- when Thomas saw Jesus, he believed;
- we have not touched Jesus but we can believe in the evidence of others.

ACTIVITIES

- Play a touching game. Pass around objects inside bags, asking the children to identify them by touch.

- Assemble an assortment of objects which can be identified by touch. Arrange to blindfold a member of the church congregation and ask him or her to identify these objects.

- Act out the discussion between the disciples and Thomas, followed by Thomas's meeting with Jesus.

- Write a letter from Thomas to a friend, telling of his experience with the risen Jesus.

DISPLAY

- Today's theme is the risen Jesus.
- Thomas wanted to touch Jesus in order to believe.
- We have not touched Jesus but we believe he lives.
- Jesus appeared to the disciples.
- Our work today is about touching.

EXPLORING WITH ADULTS

EXPERIENCE

- What are your experiences of 'touching is believing'?
- When have you believed something without touching?
- Is it possible to test everything by touching for yourself?

GOSPEL

- What does this gospel say about touching Jesus?

- How do you interpret this message for today?
- What do you understand by Thomas putting his hand in Jesus' side?

APPLICATION

- How should the church respond to the request to touch Jesus today?
- What should you say to people who want to touch Jesus for themselves?
- How should the church proclaim the physical resurrection of Jesus?

CELEBRATING TOGETHER

WELCOMING CHILDREN

At an appropriate point in the service, invite the children to present their work on touching. If the children have assembled an assortment of objects which can be identified by touch, invite a member of the congregation to be blindfolded and to identify the objects by touch, to demonstrate how we recognize things by touching them for ourselves.

HYMNS AND SONGS

Come and Praise
  18 He gave me eyes so I could see
  38 Now thank we all our God

Hymns Ancient and Modern New Standard
  82 Jesus lives! thy terrors now
145 Come, ye faithful, raise the anthem

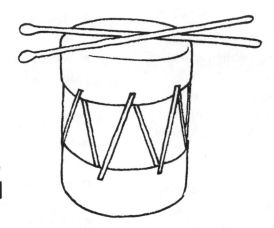

69
HEARING

GOSPEL THEME

The risen Jesus (John 20.19–31)

John's gospel portrays Jesus coming and standing among his disciples on the evening of Easter Day. Thomas, who was not present when Jesus came, refused to believe without proper evidence. A week later (the second Sunday of Easter) Jesus came and stood among his disciples again. This time Thomas was there and Jesus provided him with the evidence he needed. Thomas saw and heard and touched the risen Jesus, and then he believed. But Jesus said 'Blessed are those who have not seen and yet have come to believe'.

We can begin to share Thomas's concern for evidence by exploring the importance we attach to hearing things for ourselves.

AIMS

- to build on our experiences of hearing things and people;
- to help us understand Thomas's quest to hear for himself;
- to help us believe although we have not heard the risen Jesus.

STARTING

Whisper a message to the children. Discuss this, drawing out ideas of:

- how well they could hear the message;
- how children felt if they had difficulty hearing it;
- the importance of hearing;
- times the children have had problems because they could not hear;
- the saying 'hearing is believing'.

TALKING POINTS

Tell the story from John of the resurrection appearance. As you work, talk with the children about the significance of this. You could include the following points:

- the disciples spoke with Jesus and believed he was risen;
- Thomas was not there and did not believe;
- he needed evidence of Jesus before he would believe;
- when Thomas saw and heard Jesus, he believed;
- we have not heard Jesus but we can believe in the evidence of others.

ACTIVITIES

- Record some 'mystery voices' from television, radio or members of the congregation. Prepare to play these back in the service for people to guess the identities.

- Play a game of 'whispers'. Stand the children in a line and whisper a message down the line. See how accurate the message is by the end.

- Often the expression in our voices is as important as the words. Practise saying each of the speeches in the Bible passage, trying out different expressions to see which you think is most realistic.

- Make a mural of common sounds we hear. Discuss what these sounds tell us.

DISPLAY

- Today's theme is the risen Jesus.
- Thomas met Jesus and believed.
- We have not heard Jesus but we believe he lives.
- Jesus appeared to the disciples.
- Our work today is about hearing.

EXPLORING WITH ADULTS

EXPERIENCE

- What are your experiences of 'hearing is believing'?
- When have you believed something without hearing?
- Is it possible to test everything by hearing for yourself?

GOSPEL

- What does this gospel say about hearing Jesus?

- How do you interpret this message for today?
- What do you understand by Jesus' words to Thomas?

APPLICATION

- How should the church respond to the request to hear Jesus today?
- What should you say to people who want to hear Jesus for themselves?
- How should the church proclaim the physical resurrection of Jesus?

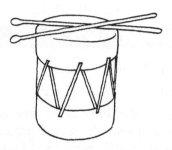

CELEBRATING TOGETHER

WELCOMING CHILDREN

At an appropriate point in the service, invite the children to present their work on hearing. If a recording has been made of different 'mystery voices' (media personalities or people in the congregation), these can be played as a quiz during the ministry of the word to demonstrate how we recognize people by hearing them for ourselves.

HYMNS AND SONGS

Come and Praise
   18 He gave me eyes so I could see
   58 At the name of Jesus

Hymns Ancient and Modern New Standard
157 Breathe on me, Breath of God
245 Jesus, these eyes have never seen

70
SHARING BREAD

PREPARATION

GOSPEL THEME

The journey to Emmaus (Luke 24.13–35)

The key to the story about the journey to Emmaus concerns the way in which the two travellers eventually recognized Jesus for who he is. Jesus was recognized in one of the very ordinary events of life, sharing bread. But at the same time Jesus gave this ordinary event extra-ordinary significance by those characteristic four actions seen at the feeding of the five thousand at the last supper. Jesus took the bread, blessed, broke it and gave it to them.

We can begin to experience the significance of Luke's teaching about the bread by exploring our own everyday experiences of sharing bread.

AIMS

- to build on our experiences of sharing bread;
- to help us understand the experience at Emmaus;
- to see Jesus in the sharing of bread.

EXPLORING WITH CHILDREN

STARTING

Bring in some bread rolls or a loaf of bread. Discuss these, drawing out ideas of:

- the children's favourite types of bread;
- times the children eat bread (such as breakfast or lunch);
- times when they share bread with others;
- any meals with bread they especially remember;
- Jesus shared bread with his disciples.

TALKING POINTS

Tell the story from Luke of the journey to Emmaus. As you work, talk with the children about the significance of this. You could include the following points:

- the disciples did not recognize Jesus;
- they invited him to stay with them;
- he took bread, blessed and broke it and gave it to them;
- he had done this when feeding the five thousand and at the last supper;
- they recognized Jesus.

ACTIVITIES

- Using prepared bread dough, shape small bread rolls to share with the congregation. These can cook during the service.
- Produce a drama about the journey to Emmaus.
- Draw a large picture of Jesus (by drawing around one of the children) holding the bread. Colour him or add paper or fabric clothes.
- Together make a book about sharing bread, with a different page for each occasion you can think of.

DISPLAY

- Today's theme is the journey to Emmaus.
- The disciples saw Jesus on the road to Emmaus.
- Jesus shared bread with his disciples.
- We remember Jesus when we share bread.
- Our work today is about sharing bread.

EXPLORING WITH ADULTS

EXPERIENCE

- What are your experiences of sharing bread?
- Have you any special memories of sharing bread?
- What is your image of Jesus sharing bread?

GOSPEL

- What does this gospel say about Jesus' way of sharing bread?
- How do you interpret this message for today?
- What do you understand by 'then their eyes were opened'?

APPLICATION

- How should the church be involved in sharing bread?
- How should you be involved in sharing bread?
- How should the Emmaus theme be developed in liturgy?

CELEBRATING TOGETHER

WELCOMING CHILDREN

At an appropriate point in the service, invite the children to present their work on sharing bread. If they have produced a drama about the journey to Emmaus, this can be shared after the gospel reading.

HYMNS AND SONGS

Come and Praise
- 27 There's a man in the streets
- 75 I saw the man from Galilee

Hymns Ancient and Modern New Standard
- 83 Love's redeeming work is done
- 412 O Lord, we long to see your face

71
EATING FISH

PREPARATION

GOSPEL THEME

Jesus eats with the disciples (Luke 24.36b–48)

The key to the story about the risen Jesus meeting with his disciples concerns the way in which they eventually recognize and accept his risen presence with them. Jesus was recognized as more than a ghost through one of the very ordinary events of life, eating fish. Here after the resurrection is clear continuity with the way things were before the crucifixion.

We can begin to experience the significance of Luke's teaching about Jesus eating with the disciples by exploring our own everyday experiences of eating fish.

AIMS

- to build on our experiences of eating fish;
- to help us understand the experience of the disciples;
- to see Jesus in the sharing of food.

EXPLORING WITH CHILDREN

STARTING

Bring in some fish, perhaps a tin of salmon. Discuss this, drawing out ideas of:

- fish the children eat;
- which fish they enjoy eating;
- how the fish is cooked;
- which meals they have fish for;
- Jesus ate broiled fish with his disciples.

TALKING POINTS

Tell the story from Luke of Jesus eating with the disciples. As you work, talk with the children about the significance of this. You could include the following points:

- the disciples were in Jerusalem;
- Jesus came to them but they thought he was a ghost;
- Jesus said to look at him and touch him;
- he asked for some fish and ate it;
- the disciples knew Jesus was alive.

ACTIVITIES

- Make a display of all the different types of fish we eat. It can include cans of fish, magazine pictures and pictures drawn by the children.
- Produce a drama about Jesus appearing to his disciples and eating fish.
- Prepare menu cards detailing your favourite fish meals and what you would eat with them.
- The disciples recognized Jesus when they shared food. We can remember him then too. Write your own meal-time prayers, remembering Jesus.

DISPLAY

- Today's theme is Jesus eating with the disciples.
- Jesus ate fish with his disciples.
- Jesus shared food with his disciples.
- We remember Jesus when we share food.
- Our work today is about eating fish.

EXPLORING WITH ADULTS

EXPERIENCE

- What are your experiences of eating fish?
- Have you any special memories of eating fish?
- What is your image of Jesus eating fish with the disciples?

GOSPEL

- What does this gospel say about the risen Jesus?
- How do you interpret this message for today?

- What do you understand by 'then he opened their minds'?

APPLICATION

- How should the church proclaim meeting Jesus in everyday things?
- How should you proclaim meeting Jesus in everyday things?
- What emphasis should the church give to these ordinary resurrection appearances?

CELEBRATING TOGETHER

WELCOMING CHILDREN

At an appropriate point in the service, invite the children to present their work on eating fish. If they have produced a drama about Jesus appearing to his disciples and eating fish with them, this can be shared after the gospel reading.

HYMNS AND SONGS

Come and Praise
  55 Colours of day dawn into the mind
129 Jesus in the garden

Hymns Ancient and Modern New Standard
349 Come, risen Lord, and deign to be our guest
424 The first day of the week

72
HAVING BREAKFAST

PREPARATION

GOSPEL THEME

The Lakeside breakfast (John 21.1–19)

The key to the story about Jesus' appearance at the lakeside concerns the way in which the disciples eventually recognized Jesus for who he is. Jesus was recognized in one of the very ordinary events of life, having breakfast. Here after the resurrection is clear continuity with the way things were before the crucifixion.

We can begin to experience the significance of John's teaching about Jesus breakfasting with his disciples by exploring our own everyday experiences of preparing and having breakfast.

AIMS

- to build on our experiences of having breakfast;
- to help us understand the experiences of the disciples at the lakeside;
- to see Jesus in the sharing of food.

EXPLORING WITH CHILDREN

STARTING

Bring in a packet of breakfast cereal. Discuss this, drawing out ideas of:

- the children's favourite cereal;
- what the children eat for breakfast;
- where they eat breakfast;
- the people with whom they eat breakfast;
- Jesus had a breakfast of fish with his disciples.

TALKING POINTS

Tell the story from John of the lakeside breakfast. As you work, talk with the children about the significance of this. You could include the following points:

- the disciples were fishing but had not caught anything;
- a man told them where to throw their nets;
- they caught 153 large fish;
- they recognized Jesus;
- Jesus shared their breakfast with them.

ACTIVITIES

- Make a poster with pictures of different breakfast foods.
- Produce a drama of the disciples fishing and later eating breakfast with Jesus.
- Bring in a toaster. Prepare toast with a variety of toppings.
- Make books in the shape of a fish or a bread roll and write in them an account of Jesus' meeting with the disciples.

DISPLAY

- Today's theme is the lakeside breakfast.
- Jesus shared breakfast with his disciples.
- The disciples recognized the risen Jesus.
- We can remember Jesus when we share food.
- Our work today is about having breakfast.

EXPLORING WITH ADULTS

EXPERIENCE

- What are your experiences of having breakfast?
- Have you any special memories of having breakfast?
- What is your image of Jesus having breakfast by the lakeside?

GOSPEL

- What does this gospel say about the breakfast of bread and fish?
- How do you interpret this message for today?
- What do you understand by 'Come and have breakfast'?

APPLICATION

- How should the church proclaim meeting Jesus in everyday things?
- How should you proclaim meeting Jesus in everyday things?
- What emphasis should the church give to these ordinary resurrection appearances?

CELEBRATING TOGETHER

WELCOMING CHILDREN

At an appropriate point in the service, invite the children to present their work on having breakfast. Invite the congregation to stay after the service to share a light breakfast, say rolls and marmalade.

HYMNS AND SONGS

Come and Praise
19 He's got the whole world, in his hands
129 Jesus in the garden

Hymns Ancient and Modern New Standard
254 Thee we adore, O hidden Saviour, thee
410 O Holy Father, God most dear

73 SHEEP

PREPARATION

GOSPEL THEME

The good shepherd (John 10.1–10)

The image of the relationship between the shepherd and the sheep to model the relationship between God and the people of God was already well established in the Old Testament, as in Psalm 23, for example. Throughout chapter 10 of his gospel John develops this image to express who Jesus is. The theme reaches its climax in verse 11 with Jesus claiming 'I am the good shepherd'. This image has inspired many generations of Christians.

We can begin to experience the significance of the image of the good shepherd by exploring our own experiences and images of sheep.

AIMS

- to build on our experiences and images of sheep;
- to help us understand Jesus as the good shepherd;
- to follow Jesus as our good shepherd.

EXPLORING WITH CHILDREN

STARTING

Bring in a picture of a sheep or a toy sheep. Discuss this, drawing out ideas of:

- the children's own experiences of sheep;
- times they have seen sheep on television;
- what they know about sheep;
- sheep are cared for by a shepherd;
- Jesus is described as the good shepherd.

TALKING POINTS

Tell Jesus' words from John of the needs of the sheep. As you work, talk with the children about the significance of this. You could include the following points:

- we are like sheep in the sheepfold;
- the sheep hear the voice of the shepherd and follow him;
- they will not follow a stranger;
- a stranger comes to steal and kill and destroy;
- Jesus comes to give life.

ACTIVITIES

- Make badges in the shape of sheep, enough to give to everyone in the congregation to demonstrate that all belong to one fold.

- Create a dance of sheep fleeing from a stranger and flocking towards the shepherd.

- Make a wall display of sheep in the sheep-fold. You could use a template to cut out the sheep but decorate each one individually.

- Make posters to take home as a reminder of Jesus, the good shepherd.

DISPLAY

- Today's theme is the good shepherd.
- Jesus is the good shepherd.
- We can follow Jesus as our shepherd.
- We are like Jesus' flock of sheep.
- Our work today is about sheep.

EXPLORING WITH ADULTS

EXPERIENCE

- What are your experiences or images of sheep?

- Where have you met the image of sheep in churches?

- How useful is the image of sheep today?

GOSPEL

- What does this gospel say about sheep?

- How do you interpret this message for today?

- What do you understand by 'I came that they may have life'?

APPLICATION

- How should the church use the image of sheep today?

- How should you use the image of sheep today?

- Should the church develop another image today in place of sheep?

CELEBRATING TOGETHER

WELCOMING CHILDREN

At an appropriate point in the service, invite the children to present their work on sheep. If enough badges have been made, these can be distributed to the whole congregation to demonstrate that they all belong to the same fold.

HYMNS AND SONGS

Come and Praise
- 53 Peace, perfect peace, is the gift of Christ our Lord
- 73 When your father made the world

Hymns Ancient and Modern New Standard
- 347 Christ, who knows all his sheep
- 382 Jesus our Lord, our King and our God

74
SHEPHERD

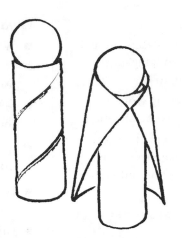

PREPARATION

GOSPEL THEME

The good shepherd (John 10.11–18)

The image of the relationship between the shepherd and the sheep to model the relationship between God and the people of God was already well established in the Old Testament, as in Psalm 23, for example. Throughout chapter 10 of his gospel John develops this image to express who Jesus is. The theme reaches its climax in verse 11 with Jesus claiming 'I am the good shepherd'. This image has inspired many generations of Christians.

We can begin to experience the significance of the image of the good shepherd by exploring our own experiences and images of the shepherd.

AIMS

● to build on our experiences and images of the shepherd;
● to help us understand Jesus as the good shepherd;
● to follow Jesus as our shepherd.

EXPLORING WITH CHILDREN

STARTING

Bring in a toy sheep or a picture of a shepherd. Discuss this, drawing out ideas of:

● the children's own experiences of shepherds;
● times they have seen shepherds on television;
● what they know about the work of shepherds;
● the risks of life for a shepherd;
● Jesus is described as the good shepherd.

TALKING POINTS

Tell Jesus' words from John about the good shepherd. As you work, talk with the children about the significance of this. You could include the following points:

● Jesus is like the good shepherd;
● we are like Jesus' sheep;
● the good shepherd protects his sheep;
● a hired servant runs away from danger;
● Jesus was ready to die for his people.

ACTIVITIES

- Make shepherd staffs from garden canes or cardboard rolls or rolled-up newspaper.
- Draw around one of the children to make a large shepherd. Paint it or dress it in paper clothes.
- Make a wall display of a shepherd and sheep, with the title 'Jesus is the good shepherd'.
- Use construction materials to make a model of a sheep farm.

DISPLAY

- Today's theme is the good shepherd.
- Jesus is the good shepherd.
- We can follow Jesus as our shepherd.
- Jesus came to die for his sheep.
- Our work today is about shepherds.

EXPLORING WITH ADULTS

EXPERIENCE

- What are your experiences or images of shepherds?
- Where have you met the image of the shepherd in churches?
- How useful is the image of the shepherd today?

GOSPEL

- What does this gospel say about the shepherd?
- How do you interpret this message for today?
- What do you understand by 'there will be one flock'?

APPLICATION

- How should the church use the image of the shepherd today?
- How should you use the image of the shepherd today?
- Should the church develop another image today in place of the shepherd?

CELEBRATING TOGETHER

WELCOMING CHILDREN

At an appropriate point in the service, invite the children to present their work on shepherds. If they have made shepherds' staffs, invite them to join the gospel procession and to hold these staffs during the gospel reading.

HYMNS AND SONGS

Come and Praise
  54 The King of Love my shepherd is
108 The Lord, the Lord, the Lord is my shepherd

Hymns Ancient and Modern New Standard
162 Jesus, where'er thy people meet
416 Praise the Lord, rise up rejoicing

75
SHEEPDOG

PREPARATION

GOSPEL THEME

The good shepherd (John 10.22–30)

The image of the relationship between the shepherd and the sheep to model the relationship between God and the people of God was already well established in the Old Testament, as in Psalm 23, for example. Throughout chapter 10 of his gospel John develops this image to express who Jesus is. The theme reaches its climax in verse 11 with Jesus claiming 'I am the good shepherd'. This image has inspired many generations of Christians.

We can begin to experience the significance of the image of the good shepherd by exploring our own experiences and images of the relationship between the shepherd and the sheepdog.

AIMS

- to build on our experiences and images of the sheepdog;
- to help us understand Jesus as the good shepherd;
- to follow Jesus as our shepherd.

EXPLORING WITH CHILDREN

STARTING

Bring in a toy dog and sheep or a picture of a sheepdog. Discuss this, drawing out ideas of:

- the children's own experiences of sheepdogs;
- times they have seen sheepdogs on television;
- what they know about the work of sheepdogs;
- why shepherds need sheepdogs;
- Jesus is described as the good shepherd.

TALKING POINTS

Tell Jesus' words from John about his sheep. As you work, talk with the children about the significance of this. You could include the following points:

- Jesus said that his followers are like his sheep;
- Jesus' sheep recognize his voice;
- Jesus knows his sheep and they follow him;
- Jesus gives eternal life to his followers;
- Jesus protects his followers.

ACTIVITIES

- Devise a dance of sheepdogs at work herding the sheep.
- Make bookmarks about Jesus the good shepherd.
- Make a wall display including sheep, shepherd and sheepdogs.
- Write guidelines for shepherds and sheepdogs about the care of sheep.

DISPLAY

- Today's theme is the good shepherd.
- Jesus is the good shepherd.
- We can follow Jesus as our shepherd.
- We are like Jesus' flock of sheep.
- Our work today is about sheepdogs.

EXPLORING WITH ADULTS

EXPERIENCE

- What are your experiences or images of sheepdogs?
- Where have you met the image of the sheepdog in churches?
- How useful is the image of the sheepdog today?

GOSPEL

- What does this gospel say about the sheep?
- How do you interpret this message for today?
- What do you understand by 'my sheep hear my voice'?

APPLICATION

- How should the church use the image of the sheep today?
- How should you use the image of the sheep today?
- Should the church develop another image today in place of the sheep?

CELEBRATING TOGETHER

WELCOMING CHILDREN

At an appropriate point in the service, invite the children to present their work on sheepdogs. If a set of slides or a video has been obtained showing sheepdogs at work, these can be shown before the gospel reading. If the children have prepared a dance about sheepdogs at work, this can be shared after the gospel reading.

HYMNS AND SONGS

Come and Praise
54 The King of Love my shepherd is
56 The Lord's my shepherd, I'll not want

Hymns Ancient and Modern New Standard
110 The God of love my shepherd is
234 Thine for ever! God of love

76 MAPS

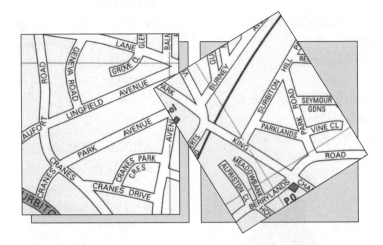

GOSPEL THEME

The way (John 14.1–14)

The image of the journey is of great importance in John's gospel, right from chapter 1 when the first disciples followed Jesus to see where Jesus was staying. Now in the present passage John shows how the journey itself is of greater significance than the destination. Jesus takes to himself the description 'I am the way'. Subsequent generations of Christians have known themselves as people of the way.

We can begin to experience the significance of Jesus as the way by exploring our own perceptions of journeys and maps.

AIMS

● to build on our experiences of maps;
● to help us understand Jesus as the way;
● to follow Jesus as the way.

STARTING

Bring in a map or street directory which includes the local area. Discuss this, drawing out ideas of:

● times the children have used maps themselves;
● using the index to find a street;
● actually looking for the children's homes;
● following a route from home to church or school;
● maps show us the way.

TALKING POINTS

Tell Jesus' words from John about being the way. As you work, talk with the children about the significance of this. You could include the following points:

● Jesus said 'I am the way… to the Father';
● the disciples asked to be shown God;
● Jesus said that whoever had seen him had seen God;
● we believe that Jesus is the way to God;
● we can follow Jesus today.

ACTIVITIES

- Produce large posters of maps showing the local area or showing the way from home to church or school.
- Make a map of Palestine in Jesus' day, showing the places he visited.
- Compose some music with one sound being echoed by others, as though it is showing the way.
- Make signs in the shape of a pointing hand or signpost to suspend from a doorway or window saying *Jesus said 'I am the way'*.

DISPLAY

- Today's theme is the way.
- Jesus said 'I am the way'.
- Maps show us the way we want to go.
- Jesus shows us the way to God.
- Our work today is about maps.

EXPLORING WITH ADULTS

EXPERIENCE

- What are your experiences of maps?
- Has a map ever been of particular help to you?
- How helpful is the map as an image for Jesus?

GOSPEL

- What does this gospel say about Jesus as the way?
- How do you interpret this message for today?
- What kind of answer does Jesus give to Thomas's question?

APPLICATION

- How should the church proclaim Jesus as the way today?
- How should you respond to Jesus as the way today?
- Should the church develop another image today in place of the way?

CELEBRATING TOGETHER

WELCOMING CHILDREN

At an appropriate point in the service, invite the children to present their work on maps. If they have produced large posters of maps, these can be displayed during the gospel reading.

HYMNS AND SONGS

Come and Praise
  42 Travel on, travel on, there's a river that is flowing
  44 He who would valiant be

Hymns Ancient and Modern New Standard
128 Thou art the Way: by thee alone
234 Thine for ever! God of love

77 VINES

PREPARATION

GOSPEL THEME

The vine (John 15.1–8)

In the Old Testament the people of Israel are described as God's vine. God planted the vine and expects fruit from the vine. John's gospel develops the image of Jesus as the true vine nurturing the branches. Those who are part of that true vine bear much fruit. Those who are not part of that true vine cannot bear fruit. The vine symbolizes the source of life.

We can begin to experience the significance of Jesus as the true vine by exploring our own experiences and images of how vines grow and develop.

AIMS

- to build on our images and experiences of vines;
- to help us understand Jesus as the true vine;
- to be nurtured in Jesus as the true vine.

EXPLORING WITH CHILDREN

STARTING

Bring in a bunch of grapes or a picture of vines. Eat the grapes and discuss, drawing out ideas of:

- the children's enjoyment of grapes;
- places where grapes grow;
- how the vines are cared for;
- the many branches growing from one vine;
- Jesus described himself as the vine with us as branches.

TALKING POINTS

Tell Jesus' words from John about the vine. As you work, talk with the children about the significance of this. You could include the following points:

- Jesus is the vine and we are the branches;
- the grapevine gives life to the branches;
- Jesus is the source of life for Christians;
- we need Jesus if we are to live a Christian life;
- the vine belongs to the vinegrower and we belong to God.

ACTIVITIES

- Make bookmarks decorated with a grapevine on one side and Jesus' words on the other.
- Paint pictures of the products we get from vines, such as grapes, sultanas, raisins, wine.
- Produce a dance of the grapevine, with healthy branches attached to the central vine and unhealthy branches letting go.
- Paint a large vine with many branches. On each branch glue a photo or put a name label showing a member of the church.

DISPLAY

- Today's theme is the vine.
- Jesus said 'I am the true vine'.
- We are branches of the true vine.
- The vine is a symbol of life.
- Our work today is about vines.

EXPLORING WITH ADULTS

EXPERIENCE

- What are your experiences of vines?
- What is distinctive about vines?
- How helpful is the vine as an image for Jesus?

GOSPEL

- What does this gospel say about Jesus as the vine?
- How do you interpret this message for today?
- What do you understand by 'those who abide in me'?

APPLICATION

- How should the church proclaim Jesus as the vine today?
- How should you respond to Jesus as the vine today?
- Should the church develop another image today in place of the vine?

CELEBRATING TOGETHER

WELCOMING CHILDREN

At an appropriate point in the service, invite the children to present their work on vines. After the gospel reading invite the whole congregation to join hands with the children to represent one huge vine stretching round the whole church.

HYMNS AND SONGS

Come and Praise
- 9 Fill your hearts with joy
- 51 Our Father, who art in heaven

Hymns Ancient and Modern New Standard
- 82 Jesus lives! thy terrors now
- 357 Father, we thank thee who hast planted

78 HEARTS

PREPARATION

GOSPEL THEME

The new commandment (John 13.31–35)

In the synoptic gospels Jesus is portrayed as summing up the law of Moses in terms of the two great commandments, to love God and to love your neighbour as yourself. Here in John's gospel Jesus gives his followers a new commandment, that they love one another. This new commandment has been characterized as the essence of the Christian way of life.

We can begin to experience the significance of this new commandment by exploring some of our own images and expressions of love. The heart has become the key symbol of love.

AIMS

● to build on our images and experiences of the heart;
● to help us grasp the significance of the new commandment;
● to respond to the new commandment to love one another.

EXPLORING WITH CHILDREN

STARTING

Bring in a greeting card which shows a heart as a symbol of love. Discuss this, drawing out ideas of:

● we use the heart to show our love;
● cards the children have sent which use hearts this way;
● cards like this that the children have received;
● other items which use hearts in this way;
● Jesus told us to love one another.

TALKING POINTS

Tell Jesus' words from John about the new commandment. As you work, talk with the children about the significance of this. You could include the following points:

● the people of God had many commandments to follow;
● Jesus gave a new one;
● Jesus said we should love one another;
● we are to love just as Jesus loves us;
● the followers of Jesus should be recognized by their love.

ACTIVITIES

- Make large heart-shaped banners.
- Construct cardboard hangers to go over a doorknob. Write on them Jesus' words. Encourage the children to display these in their rooms as a reminder to love one another.
- Write poems about love.
- Bake biscuits in the shape of hearts. Share these with the congregation.

DISPLAY

- Today's theme is the new commandment.
- Jesus told us to love one another.
- We should love as Jesus loves us.
- Jesus' followers are known by their love.
- Our work today is about hearts.

EXPLORING WITH ADULTS

EXPERIENCE

- What are your experiences of hearts as a symbol for love?
- Have you ever been particularly moved by a heart?
- How helpful is the heart as an image for the church?

GOSPEL

- What does this gospel say about love?
- How do you interpret this message for today?
- What do you understand by 'just as I have loved you'?

APPLICATION

- How should the church proclaim the new commandment today?
- How should you proclaim the new commandment today?
- How should the worship of the church display love?

CELEBRATING TOGETHER

WELCOMING CHILDREN

At an appropriate point in the service, invite the children to present their work on hearts as a symbol for love. If the children have made large heart-shaped banners, these can be carried in the gospel procession and held high during the gospel reading.

HYMNS AND SONGS

Come and Praise
  99 Love will never come to an end
101 In the bustle of the city

Hymns Ancient and Modern New Standard
374 Help us to help each other, Lord
465 God is love, and where true love is

79
THE GUIDE

PREPARATION

GOSPEL THEME

The Paraclete (John 14.15–21)

When Jesus is preparing his disciples for this ongoing life in the world after he has been taken from them, he promises them that the Father will give another *Paraclete* to be with them for ever. This word 'Paraclete' is peculiar to the Johannine literature. The usual translation 'Advocate' refers to someone who argues our case on our behalf. Literally the word means 'someone called to our side'. In some senses the Paraclete is our guide.

We can begin to experience the significance of John's teaching about the Paraclete by exploring our own experiences of the guide.

AIMS

- to build on our experiences of the guide;
- to help us understand John's reference to the Paraclete;
- to be aware of the Paraclete's support.

EXPLORING WITH CHILDREN

STARTING

Explain that you want one child to move to a different seat. With words, guide the child forward, left or right, specifying the number of steps. Discuss this experience, drawing out ideas of:

- how the child felt at being guided;
- how well you guided the child;
- experiences the children have had of being guided by another;
- other times when guidance is needed;
- Jesus promised the Holy Spirit as a guide.

TALKING POINTS

Tell Jesus' words from John about the Paraclete, or guide. As you work, talk with the children about the significance of this. You could include the following points:

- Jesus warned his disciples that he would leave them;
- he promised God would send them help;
- this helper would be like a guide;
- this guide is the Holy Spirit;
- the Holy Spirit still guides us today.

ACTIVITIES

- Use any maps prepared in the previous session and write a guide on how to get from one place to another.
- Prepare a dance about a guide leading others in various actions and in different directions.
- Write a thank-you prayer about the Holy Spirit, our Guide.
- Take turns guiding each other around by spoken instructions. (Do not blindfold the one being guided, as this is not necessarily safe with children.)

DISPLAY

- Today's theme is the Paraclete.
- Jesus promised a guide.
- The Holy Spirit is our guide.
- Thank you for the Holy Spirit, our guide.
- Our work today is about the guide.

EXPLORING WITH ADULTS

EXPERIENCE

- What are your experiences of a guide?
- Have you ever been a guide?
- How useful is the image of the guide to understand the Holy Spirit?

GOSPEL

- What does this gospel say about the Paraclete?
- How do you interpret this message for today?
- What do you understand by 'he abides with you, and he will be in you'?

APPLICATION

- How should the church act as a guide today?
- How should you act as a guide today?
- How should the image of the guide be used in liturgy?

CELEBRATING TOGETHER

WELCOMING CHILDREN

At an appropriate point in the service, invite the children to present their work on the guide. If the children have prepared a dance about the guide, this can be shared after the gospel reading.

HYMNS AND SONGS

Come and Praise
  62 Heavenly Father, may thy blessing
 107 You've got to move when the Spirit says move

Hymns Ancient and Modern New Standard
 156 Come down, O Love divine
 157 Breathe on me, Breath of God

80
THE TEAM

GOSPEL THEME

The Christian community (John 15.9–17)

When Jesus is preparing his disciples for their ongoing life in the world after he has been taken from them, he makes two important points. He calls them his friends and he gives them the commandment to love one another as he has loved them. The group of people whom Jesus leaves behind are to be united as a team bound together in mutual love.

We can begin to experience the significance of Jesus' teaching about the quality of life among his followers by exploring our understanding of good teams.

AIMS

- to build on our experiences of good teams;
- to help us understand Jesus' followers as a team;
- to want to be part of that mutually supportive team.

EXPLORING WITH CHILDREN

STARTING

Bring in a picture or T-shirt or newspaper cutting of your favourite team. Discuss this, drawing out ideas of:

- the children's favourite teams;
- teams the children are in;
- different types of teams in the world;
- the way that teams need to work together;
- Jesus said his followers were to be like a team.

TALKING POINTS

Tell Jesus' words from John about the Christian community. As you work, talk with the children about the significance of this. You could include the following points:

- Jesus reminded his followers that he loved them;
- Jesus told his followers to love one another;
- he said to love as he loved them;
- when we love each other we are friends of Jesus;
- we are like a team joined together by love.

ACTIVITIES

- Prepare pictures of your favourite teams, ready for a display.

- We are all part of Jesus' team. Make a team emblem for each person, such as a badge or an armband.

- Produce two static tableaux to compare. The first is of a group of people facing away from each other and ignoring each other. The second is of a team of people working together.

- Cut out strings of connecting paper dolls from paper folded fanwise. Decorate each one differently. Jesus' followers are all different but joined together in love.

DISPLAY

- Today's theme is the Christian community.
- Jesus told his followers to love one another.
- We are in Jesus' team.
- Love binds us into a team.
- Our work today is about the team.

EXPLORING WITH ADULTS

EXPERIENCE

- What are your experiences of teams?
- Have you ever been part of a really good team?
- How useful is the image of the team to understand the church?

GOSPEL

- What does this gospel say about the followers of Jesus?
- How do you interpret this message for today?

- What do you understand by 'I have called you friends'?

APPLICATION

- How should the church be seen as a team today?
- How should you contribute to that team today?
- How should the image of the team be used in liturgy?

CELEBRATING TOGETHER

WELCOMING CHILDREN

At an appropriate point in the service, invite the children to present their work on the team. If the children have prepared pictures of their favourite teams, these can be displayed during the gospel reading.

HYMNS AND SONGS

Come and Praise
   20 Come, my brothers, praise the Lord
   30 Join with us to sing God's praises

Hymns Ancient and Modern New Standard
   161 Christ is our corner-stone
   170 The Church's one foundation

81
THE COACH

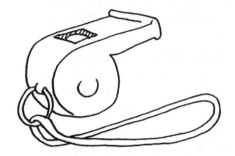

GOSPEL THEME

The Paraclete (John 14.23–29)

When Jesus is preparing his disciples for this ongoing life in the world after he has been taken from them, he promises them that the Father will give another *Paraclete* to be with them for ever. This word 'Paraclete' is peculiar to the Johannine literature. The usual translation 'Advocate' refers to someone who argues our case on our behalf. Literally the word means 'someone called to our side'. In this passage Jesus promises that the Paraclete 'will teach you everything and remind you of all that I have said to you'. In some senses the Paraclete is our coach.

We can begin to experience the significance of John's teaching about the Paraclete by exploring our own experiences of the coach.

AIMS

- to build on our experiences of the coach;
- to help us understand John's reference to the Paraclete;
- to be aware of the Paraclete's support.

STARTING

Bring in a symbol of a coach, such as a whistle. Discuss this, drawing out ideas of:

- sports or activities that need a coach;
- the equipment used by a coach;
- the work of a coach;
- children in the group who know a coach;
- the Holy Spirit is like a coach.

TALKING POINTS

Tell Jesus' words from John about the Holy Spirit. As you work, talk with the children about the significance of this. You could include the following points:

- Jesus said his followers were to keep his words;
- he promised that God would send the Holy Spirit;
- the Holy Spirit would be like a coach;
- the Holy Spirit would help Jesus' followers remember his words;
- the Holy Spirit still coaches us today.

ACTIVITIES

Prepare a drama or mime about the work of the coach. Begin with a group that is not working well but improves when coached.

● Make cardboard and paper models of equipment needed by a modern coach.
● Interview the pastor or a member of the congregation about his or her experiences of the Holy Spirit as a coach.
● Blow up balloons and write on them a thank you to the Holy Spirit, our coach.

DISPLAY

● Today's theme is the Paraclete.
● The Holy Spirit is our coach.
● God sends the Holy Spirit to help us.
● Thank you for the Holy Spirit, our coach.
● Our work today is about the coach.

EXPLORING WITH ADULTS

EXPERIENCE

● What are your experiences of coaches?
● Have you ever been a coach?
● How useful is the image of the coach to understand the Holy Spirit?

GOSPEL

● What does this gospel say about the Paraclete?
● How do you interpret this message for today?

● What do you understand by 'the Paraclete … will teach you everything'?

APPLICATION

● How should the church act as a coach today?
● How should you act as a coach today?
● How should the image of the coach be used in liturgy?

CELEBRATING TOGETHER

WELCOMING CHILDREN

At an appropriate point in the service, invite the children to present their work on the coach. Invite a sports coach to talk about his or her work during the ministry of the word. With the children's help it will be possible to demonstrate the coach at work.

HYMNS AND SONGS

Come and Praise
   85 Spirit of peace, come to our waiting world
   96 A still small voice in the heart of the city

Hymns Ancient and Modern New Standard
   92 Come, thou Holy Spirit, come
  154 Gracious Spirit, Holy Ghost

82
ROYAL CROWNS

GOSPEL THEME

Going to the Father (John 17.1–11)

With chapter 17 John concludes Jesus' farewell discourse with the disciples over the last supper before Jesus goes out to face his arrest. In this chapter Jesus looks forward with confidence to returning to the Father. What John expresses in this farewell discourse Luke symbolizes through the ascension, which links the close of Luke's gospel with the opening of the Acts of the Apostles. The ascension, or Jesus' going to the Father, is seen as his enthronement. The ascension is also kept as the feast of Christ the King.

We can begin to experience the significance of the feast of Christ the King by exploring our own images of royal crowns.

AIMS

● to build on our images of royal crowns;
● to help us understand the ascension as the feast of Christ the King;
● to celebrate the ascended Christ.

STARTING

Bring in a crown or a picture of a monarch wearing a crown. Discuss this, drawing out ideas of:

● visits the children may have made to see the Crown Jewels;
● any pictures of crowns children have seen;
● people who wear crowns;
● a crown is a symbol of royalty;
● Jesus is our King.

TALKING POINTS

Tell Jesus' words from John about going to the Father. As you work, talk with the children about the significance of this. You could include the following points:

● at the last supper Jesus prayed;
● he asked God to glorify him;
● after he rose from death, he ascended to heaven;
● we think of this as the time Jesus became King;
● each year we celebrate Christ the King.

ACTIVITIES

- Make royal crowns.
- Prepare a tableau or mime of everyone bowing down to Jesus, as a symbol of Jesus as King.
- Bake biscuits in the shape of simple crowns.
- Make crown-shaped bookmarks with the words 'Christ the King'.

DISPLAY

- Today's theme is going to the Father.
- We celebrate Christ, our King.
- The ascension shows that Jesus is King.
- Today we celebrate Jesus' ascension.
- Our work today is about royal crowns.

EXPLORING WITH ADULTS

EXPERIENCE

- What are your images of royal crowns?
- What feelings are stirred in you by royal crowns?
- How appropriate is the image of royal crowns today?

GOSPEL

- What does this gospel say about Jesus going to the Father?
- How do you interpret this message for today?
- What do you understand by 'Father, glorify me in your presence'?

APPLICATION

- How should the church celebrate the ascension of Christ?
- How should you celebrate the ascension of Christ?
- How helpful is the imagery of ascension in liturgy?

CELEBRATING TOGETHER

WELCOMING CHILDREN

At an appropriate point in the service, invite the children to present their work on royal crowns. If the children have made royal crowns, arrange for these to be worn in the gospel procession.

HYMNS AND SONGS

Come and Praise
   37 O praise ye the Lord!
   58 At the name of Jesus

Hymns Ancient and Modern New Standard
   140 All hail the power of Jesus' name!
   262 Alleluia, sing to Jesus!

83
ROYAL ROBES

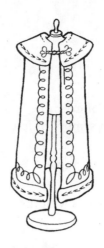

GOSPEL THEME

Going to the Father (John 17.6–19)

With chapter 17 John concludes Jesus' farewell discourse with the disciples over the last supper before Jesus goes out to face his arrest. In this chapter Jesus looks forward with confidence to returning to the Father. What John expresses in this farewell discourse Luke symbolizes through the ascension, which links the close of Luke's gospel with the opening of the Acts of the Apostles. The ascension, or Jesus' going to the Father, is seen as his enthronement. The ascension is also kept as the feast of Christ the King.

We can begin to experience the significance of the feast of Christ the King by exploring our own images of royal robes.

AIMS

● to build on our images of royal robes;
● to help us understand the ascension as the feast of Christ the King;
● to celebrate the ascended Christ.

STARTING

Bring in a theatrical cloak or a picture of royal robes from history or fairy story. Discuss this, drawing out ideas of:

● the richness of the robes;
● who wears such robes;
● when royal robes are worn (such as a coronation);
● any robes or pictures the children have seen;
● Jesus did not wear royal robes but he is our King.

TALKING POINTS

Tell Jesus' words from John about going to the Father. As you work, talk with the children about the significance of this. You could include the following points:

● at the last supper Jesus asked God to protect his followers;
● he knew he would soon die and go to be with God;
● after he rose from death, he ascended to heaven;
● we think of this as the time Jesus became King;
● each year we celebrate Christ the King.

ACTIVITIES

- Make royal robes out of old sheets and curtains.
- Compose royal processional music.
- Design and draw a variety of royal robes to display.
- Design a postage stamp to celebrate Jesus as King.

DISPLAY

- Today's theme is going to the Father.
- We celebrate Christ, our King.
- The ascension shows that Jesus is King.
- Today we celebrate Jesus' ascension.
- Our work today is about royal robes.

EXPLORING WITH ADULTS

EXPERIENCE

- What are your images of royal robes?
- What feelings are stirred in you by royal robes?
- How appropriate is the image of royal robes today?

GOSPEL

- What does this gospel say about Jesus going to the Father?
- How do you interpret this message for today?
- What do you understand by 'now I am coming to you'?

APPLICATION

- How should the church celebrate the ascension of Christ?
- How should you celebrate the ascension of Christ?
- How helpful is the imagery of ascension in liturgy?

CELEBRATING TOGETHER

WELCOMING CHILDREN

At an appropriate point in the service, invite the children to present their work on royal robes. If the children have made royal robes, arrange for them to join the gospel procession wearing their robes.

HYMNS AND SONGS

Come and Praise
- 40 Praise Him, praise Him
- 58 At the name of Jesus

Hymns Ancient and Modern New Standard
- 143 Jesus shall reign where'er the sun
- 147 Crown him with many crowns

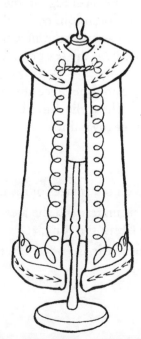

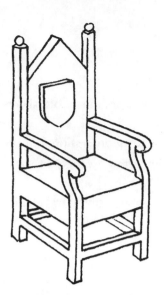

84
ROYAL THRONES

GOSPEL THEME

Going to the Father (John 17.20–26)

With chapter 17 John concludes Jesus' farewell discourse with the disciples over the last supper before Jesus goes out to face his arrest. In this chapter Jesus looks forward with confidence to returning to the Father. What John expresses in this farewell discourse Luke symbolizes through the ascension, which links the close of Luke's gospel with the opening of the Acts of the Apostles. The ascension, or Jesus' going to the Father, is seen as his enthronement. The ascension is also kept as the feast of Christ the King.

We can begin to experience the significance of the feast of Christ the King by exploring our own images of royal thrones.

AIMS

- to build on our images of royal thrones;
- to help us understand the ascension as the feast of Christ the King;
- to celebrate the ascended Christ.

STARTING

Show a picture of a royal throne, from history or from a fairy story. Discuss this, drawing out ideas of:

- any reactions the children have to the throne;
- pictures of thrones the children have seen;
- what is special about thrones;
- a royal throne is used by a king or queen;
- Jesus is our King.

TALKING POINTS

Tell Jesus' words from John about going to the Father. As you work, talk with the children about the significance of this. You could include the following points:

- at the last supper Jesus asked God to protect his followers;
- he wanted them and us to be one in him;
- he prayed for his followers to see the glory God gave him;
- after he rose from death, he ascended to heaven;
- we think of this as the time Jesus became King.

ACTIVITIES

- Prepare a royal throne by decorating a chair.
- Design small cardboard models of thrones, decorated with shiny paper, glitter and sequins.
- Decorate cards to give to others to celebrate Christ the King.
- Practise a dance of coronation or enthronement.

DISPLAY

- Today's theme is going to the Father.
- We celebrate Christ, our King.
- The ascension shows that Jesus is King.
- Today we celebrate Jesus' ascension.
- Our work today is about royal thrones.

EXPLORING WITH ADULTS

EXPERIENCE

- What are your images of royal thrones?
- What feelings are stirred in you by royal thrones?
- How appropriate is the image of royal thrones today?

GOSPEL

- What does this gospel say about Jesus going to the Father?
- How do you interpret this message for today?
- What do you understand by 'the glory that you have given me'?

APPLICATION

- How should the church celebrate the ascension of Christ?
- How should you celebrate the ascension of Christ?
- How helpful is the imagery of ascension in liturgy?

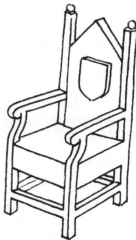

CELEBRATING TOGETHER

WELCOMING CHILDREN

At an appropriate point in the service, invite the children to present their work on royal thrones. If the children have decorated a royal throne, arrange for the gospel to be read from this throne.

HYMNS AND SONGS

Come and Praise
- 41 Fill thou my life, O Lord my God
- 58 At the name of Jesus

Hymns Ancient and Modern New Standard
- 139 Rejoice! the Lord is King
- 194 King of glory, King of peace

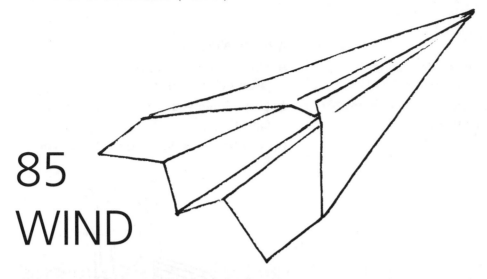

85 WIND

GOSPEL THEME

The Holy Spirit (John 20.19–23)

It is Luke who provides the foundation account for the Day of Pentecost through his narrative in the Acts of the Apostles. The Holy Spirit came to the apostles with a sound like a mighty rushing wind. John has a somewhat different account of Jesus breathing on the disciples and saying to them 'Receive the Holy Spirit'. The three ideas of wind, breath and Spirit were all very closely linked in Hebrew thought.

We can begin to experience the significance of the Bible imagery concerning the Holy Spirit by exploring our own perceptions of wind.

AIMS

- to build on our experiences of wind;
- to help us understand the wind as a model for the Holy Spirit;
- to be open to the Holy Spirit.

STARTING

Bring in some balloons and invite the children to move them around the room by blowing on them, by wind power. Discuss this, drawing out ideas of:

- how easy or difficult it was;
- how well the balloons responded to the wind;
- other things that are controlled by wind;
- the power of the wind;
- the wind is a symbol or model for the Holy Spirit.

TALKING POINTS

Tell the story from John of Jesus breathing on the disciples. As you work, talk with the children about the significance of this. You could include the following points:

- after Jesus' death the disciples were in a locked room;
- Jesus came and breathed on the disciples;
- he gave them the gift of the Holy Spirit;
- we celebrate this at Pentecost;
- the Holy Spirit is here to help us today.

ACTIVITIES

● Experiment with ways of making the sound of rushing wind, using voices, instruments and any objects possible.

● Make hand-held windmills to be powered by your breath. From each corner of a square of thin card, cut in toward the centre. Flange these blades slightly and attach the points to the centre and to a stick with a drawing pin.

● Make paper aeroplanes to use outside in the wind.

● Blow up balloons and write on them a message such as 'Come Holy Spirit'.

DISPLAY

● Today's theme is the Holy Spirit.

● At Pentecost we celebrate the coming of the Holy Spirit.

● The Holy Spirit is God's gift to us.

● The wind is a picture of the Holy Spirit.

● Our work today is about the wind.

EXPLORING WITH ADULTS

EXPERIENCE

● What are your experiences and images of the wind?

● What are the main characteristics of the wind?

● How does wind speak to you about the Holy Spirit?

GOSPEL

● What does this gospel say about the Holy Spirit?

● How do you interpret this message for today?

● What do you understand by Jesus breathing on the disciples?

APPLICATION

● How should the church celebrate the Day of Pentecost?

● How should you celebrate the Day of Pentecost?

● How can the image of wind be used in liturgy?

CELEBRATING TOGETHER

WELCOMING CHILDREN

At an appropriate point in the service, invite the children to present their work on wind. If they have prepared ways of making the sounds of rushing wind, arrange for these sounds to add dramatic effect to the gospel reading.

HYMNS AND SONGS

Come and Praise
  63 Spirit of God, as strong as the wind
  96 A still small voice in the heart of the city

Hymns Ancient and Modern New Standard
  152 O Holy Spirit, Lord of grace
  155 O Holy Ghost, thy people bless

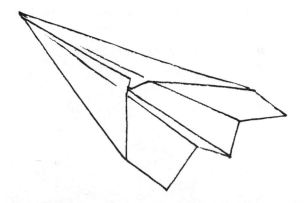

86
FIRE

GOSPEL THEME

The Holy Spirit (John 15.26–27; 16.4b–15)

It is Luke who provides the foundation account for the Day of Pentecost through his narrative in the Acts of the Apostles. The Holy Spirit came to the apostles and settled on them like tongues of fire. It is for this reason that tongues of fire have become a classic image for the Holy Spirit.

We can begin to experience the significance of the Bible imagery concerning the Holy Spirit by exploring our own perceptions of fire.

AIMS

- to build on our experiences of fire;
- to help us understand fire as a model for the Holy Spirit;
- to be open to the Holy Spirit.

EXPLORING WITH CHILDREN

STARTING

Bring in a picture of a fire. Discuss this, drawing out ideas of:

- those who have fires at home;
- times the children have experienced fire;
- the importance of fire to less developed countries;
- the power of fire;
- fire is a symbol or model for the Holy Spirit.

TALKING POINTS

Tell Jesus' words from John about the coming of the Spirit. As you work, talk with the children about the significance of this. You could include the following points:

- Jesus promised that the Holy Spirit would come;
- the Holy Spirit would guide and help the disciples;
- this happened at Pentecost;
- a symbol of the Holy Spirit's coming was tongues of fire;
- the Holy Spirit still guides and helps us today.

ACTIVITIES

- Make headdresses to represent tongues of fire settling on the disciples' heads.
- Make Pentecost cards with Cellophane flames on the front.
- Make a Pentecost banner showing tongues of flame.
- Write an acrostic about the Holy Spirit.

DISPLAY

- Today's theme is the Holy Spirit.
- At Pentecost we celebrate the coming of the Holy Spirit.
- The Holy Spirit is God's gift to us.
- Fire is a picture of the Holy Spirit.
- Our work today is about fire.

EXPLORING WITH ADULTS

EXPERIENCE

- What are your experiences and images of fire?
- What are the main characteristics of fire?
- How does fire speak to you about the Holy Spirit?

GOSPEL

- What does this gospel say about the Holy Spirit?
- How do you interpret this message for today?
- What do you understand by the Spirit guiding into all truth?

APPLICATION

- How should the church celebrate the Day of Pentecost?

- How should you celebrate the Day of Pentecost?
- How can the image of fire be used in liturgy?

CELEBRATING TOGETHER

WELCOMING CHILDREN

At an appropriate point in the service, invite the children to present their work on fire. If they have prepared headdresses to represent the tongues of fire settling on the disciples' heads, these can be worn during the gospel reading.

HYMNS AND SONGS

Come and Praise
43 Give me oil in my lamp, keep me burning
85 Spirit of peace, come to our waiting world

Hymns Ancient and Modern New Standard
503 Of all the Spirit's gifts to me
504 On the day of Pentecost

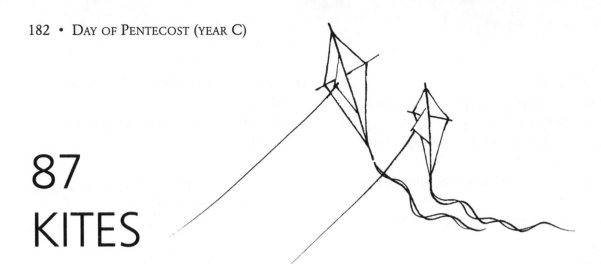

87
KITES

PREPARATION

GOSPEL THEME

The Holy Spirit (John 14.8–17)

It is Luke who provides the foundation account for the Day of Pentecost through his narrative in the Acts of the Apostles. The Holy Spirit came to the apostles with the sound of a mighty rushing wind and settled on them like tongues of fire. No one image is powerful enough to capture the nature of the Holy Spirit.

We can begin to experience the significance of the Bible imagery concerning the Holy Spirit by exploring our own perceptions of kites.

AIMS

● to build on our experiences of kites;
● to help us understand kites as a model for the Holy Spirit;
● to be open to the Holy Spirit.

EXPLORING WITH CHILDREN

STARTING

Bring in a kite. Discuss this, drawing out ideas of:

● the type of kite it is;
● kites the children have seen;
● the freedom of kites to soar in the sky;
● the mobility of kites;
● the kite as a symbol or model for the Holy Spirit.

TALKING POINTS

Tell Jesus' words from John about the coming of the Holy Spirit. As you work, talk with the children about the significance of this. You could include the following points:

● Jesus promised that the Holy Spirit would come;
● the Holy Spirit would be with the disciples forever;
● this happened at Pentecost;
● the Holy Spirit still guides and helps us today;
● one symbol we can use for the Holy Spirit is a kite.

ACTIVITIES

- Prepare a dance of flying kites.
- Fold paper kites. Borrow from your local library a book on origami to teach you how.
- Make kites to decorate the church.
- Write a prayer to the Holy Spirit.

DISPLAY

- Today's theme is the Holy Spirit.
- At Pentecost we celebrate the coming of the Holy Spirit.
- The Holy Spirit is God's gift to us.
- The kite is a picture of the Holy Spirit.
- Our work today is about kites.

EXPLORING WITH ADULTS

EXPERIENCE

- What are your experiences and images of kites?
- What are the main characteristics of kites?
- How do kites speak to you about the Holy Spirit?

GOSPEL

- What does this gospel say about the Holy Spirit?
- How do you interpret this message for today?
- What do you understand by the Spirit abiding with you?

APPLICATION

- How should the church celebrate the Day of Pentecost?

- How should you celebrate the Day of Pentecost?
- How can the image of kites be used in liturgy?

CELEBRATING TOGETHER

WELCOMING CHILDREN

At an appropriate point in the service, invite the children to present their work on kites. If they have prepared a dance about kites, this can be presented after the gospel reading.

HYMNS AND SONGS

Come and Praise
  48 Father, hear the prayer we offer
  63 Spirit of God, as strong as the wind

Hymns Ancient and Modern New Standard
  153 Come, gracious Spirit, heavenly Dove
  471 Holy Spirit, come, confirm us

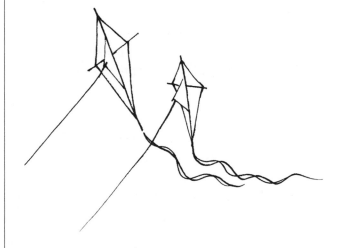